How Marxism Works
Chris Harman

Bookmarks
London, Chicago, Melbourne

How Marxism Works

Chris Harman

How Marxism Works / *Chris Harman*
Fourth edition published January 1993
Bookmarks, 265 Seven Sisters Road, London N4 2DE
Bookmarks, PO Box 16085, Chicago, Il. 60616
Bookmarks, GPO Box 1473N, Melbourne 3001
First published by the Socialist Workers Party May 1979
© Chris Harman and Bookmarks
ISBN 0 906224 78 0

Bookmarks is linked to an international grouping of socialist
organisations:
AUSTRALIA: **International Socialist Organisation**,
GPO Box 1473N, Melbourne 3001
BELGIUM: **Socialisme International**,
Rue Lovinfosse 60, 4030 Grevignée
BRITAIN: **Socialist Workers Party**,
PO Box 82, London E3 3LH
CANADA: **International Socialists**,
PO Box 339, Station E, Toronto, Ontario M6H 4E3
CYPRUS: **Workers Democracy**,
PO Box 7280, Nicosia, Cyprus
DENMARK: **Internationale Socialister**,
Ryesgade 8, 3, 8000, Århus C
FRANCE: **Socialisme International**,
BP 189, 75926 Paris, Cedex 19
GERMANY: **Sozialistische Arbeitersgruppe**,
Wolfsgangstrasse 81, W-6000, Frankfurt 1
GREECE: **Organosi Sosialistiki Epanastasi**,
PO Box 8161, 10010, Omonia, Athens
HOLLAND: **Groep Internationale Socialisten**,
PO Box 9720, 3506 GR Utrecht
IRELAND: **Socialist Workers Movement**,
PO Box 1648, Dublin 8
NORWAY: **Internasjonale Sosialister**,
Postboks 9226, Grønland 0134, Oslo
POLAND: **Solidarnosc Socjalistyczna**,
PO Box 12, 01-900 Warszawa 118
SOUTH AFRICA: **International Socialists of South Africa**,
PO Box 18530, Hillbrow 2038
UNITED STATES: **International Socialist Organisation**,
PO Box 16085, Chicago, Il. 60616

Contents

Chris Harman is a leading member of the Socialist Workers Party and editor of *Socialist Worker*. His other publications include *Class Struggles in Eastern Europe*, *The Lost Revolution: Germany 1918-1923*, *Explaining the Crisis* and *The Fire Last Time: 1968 and after*.

Introduction

THERE IS A widespread myth that Marxism is difficult. It is a myth propagated by the enemies of socialism—former Labour leader Harold Wilson boasted that he was never able to get beyond the first page of Marx's *Capital*. It is a myth also encouraged by a peculiar breed of academics who declare themselves to be 'Marxists': they deliberately cultivate obscure phrases and mystical expressions in order to give the impression that they possess a special knowledge denied to others.

So it is hardly suprising that many socialists who work 40 hours a week in factories, mines or offices take it for granted that Marxism is something they will never have the time or the opportunity to understand.

In fact the basic ideas of Marxism are remarkably simple. They explain, as no other set of ideas can, the society in which we live. They make sense of a world wracked by crises, of its poverty in the midst of plenty, of its coups d'etat and military dictatorships, of the way in which marvellous inventions can consign millions to the dole queues, of 'democracies' that subsidise torturers and of 'socialist' states that threaten each other's people with nuclear missiles.

Meanwhile, the establishment thinkers who so deride Marxist ideas chase each other round in a mad game of blind man's buff, understanding nothing and explaining less.

But though Marxism is not difficult, there *is* a problem for the reader who comes across Marx's writings for the first time. Marx wrote well over a century ago. He used the language of the time, complete with references to individuals and events then familiar to virtually everyone, now known only to specialist historians.

I remember my own bafflement when, while still at school, I tried to read his pamphlet *The 18th Brumaire of Louis Bonaparte*. I didn't know either what Brumaire was or who Louis Bonaparte was. How many socialists have abandoned attempts to come to grips with Marxism after such experiences!

This is the justification for this short book. It seeks to provide an introduction to Marxist ideas, which will make it easier for socialists to follow what Marx was on about and to understand the development of Marxism since then in the hands of Frederick Engels, Rosa Luxemburg, Vladimir Lenin, Leon Trotsky, and a whole host of lesser thinkers.

Much of this pamphlet first appeared as a series of articles in *Socialist Worker* under the title 'Marxism Made Easy'. But I have added substantial fresh material. A little of this I have lifted wholesale from two previous attempts to provide a simple exposition of Marxist ideas: Duncan Hallas's *The Meaning of Marxism* and Norwich SWP's 'Marxist Education Series'.

One final point. Space has prevented me from dealing in this pamphlet with some important parts of the Marxist analysis of the modern world. References to further reading on these are contained in the appendix.

CHRIS HARMAN

1

Why we need Marxist theory

'WHAT DO we need *theory* for? We know there is a crisis. We know we are being robbed by our employers. We know we're all angry. We know we need socialism. All the rest is just for the intellectuals.'

You often hear words such as these from militant socialists and trade unionists. Such views are strongly encouraged by anti socialists, who try to give the impression that Marxism is an obscure, complicated and boring doctrine.

Socialist ideas, they say, are 'abstract'. They may seem all right in theory, but in real life common sense tells us something else entirely.

The trouble with these arguments is that the people who put them forward usually have a 'theory' of their own, even if they refuse to recognise it. Ask them any question about society, and they will try to answer it with some generalisation or other. A few examples...

'People are naturally selfish.'

'Anyone can get to the top if they try hard enough.'

'If it weren't for the rich there wouldn't be any money to provide work for the rest of us.'

'If only we could educate the workers, society would change.'

'Declining morals have brought the country to its present state.'

Listen to any argument in the street, on the bus, in the canteen. You'll hear dozens of such sayings. Each and every one contains a view of why society is like it is and of how people can improve their condition. Such views are all 'theories' of society.

When people say they do not have a theory, all they really mean is they have not clarified their views.

This is particularly dangerous for anyone who is trying to change society. For the newspapers, the radio, the TV, are all continually filling our minds with attempted explanations for the mess society is in. They hope we will accept what they say without thinking more about the issues.

But you cannot fight effectively to change society unless you recognise what is false in all these different arguments.

This was first shown 150 years ago. In the 1830s and 1840s the development of industry in areas such as the north west of England drew hundreds of thousands of men, women and children into miserably paid jobs. They were forced to endure living conditions of unbelievable squalor.

They began to fight back against this with the first mass workers' organisations—the first trade unions, and in Britain the first movement for political rights for workers, Chartism. Alongside these movements were the first small groups of people dedicated to winning socialism.

Immediately the problem arose as to *how* the workers' movement could achieve its aim.

Some people said it was possible to persuade society's rulers to change things through peaceful means. The 'moral force' of a mass, peaceful movement would ensure that benefits were given to the workers. Hundreds of thousands of people organised, demonstrated, worked to build a movement on the basis of such views—only to end defeated and demoralised.

Others recognised the need to use 'physical force', but thought this could be achieved by fairly small, conspiratorial groups cut off from the rest of society. These too led tens of thousands of workers into struggles that ended in defeat and demoralisation.

Still others believed the workers could achieve their

goals by economic action, without confronting the army and the police. Again, their arguments led to mass actions. In England in 1842 the world's first general strike took place in the industrial areas of the north, with tens of thousands of workers holding out for four weeks until forced back to work by hunger and privation.

It was towards the end of the first stage of defeated workers' struggles, in 1848, that the German socialist, Karl Marx, spelt out his own ideas fully, in his pamphlet *The Communist Manifesto*.

His ideas were not pulled out of thin air. They attempted to provide a basis for dealing with all the questions that had been brought up by the workers' movement of the time.

The ideas Marx developed are still relevant today. It is stupid to say, as some people do, that they must be out of date because Marx first wrote them down more than 150 years ago. In fact, all the notions of society that Marx argued with are still very widespread. Just as the Chartists argued about 'moral force' or 'physical force', socialists today argue about the 'parliamentary road' or the 'revolutionary road'. Among those who are revolutionaries the argument for and against 'terrorism' is as alive as it was in 1848.

The idealists

MARX WAS not the first person to try to describe what was wrong with society. At the time he was writing, new inventions in factories were turning out wealth on a scale undreamt of by previous generations. For the first time it seemed humanity had the means to defend itself against the natural calamities that had been the scourge of previous ages.

Yet this did not mean any improvement in the lives of the majority of the people. Quite the opposite. The men, women and children who manned the new factories led lives much worse that those led by their grandparents who had toiled the land. Their wages barely kept them above the bread line; periodic bouts of mass unemployment thrust them well below it.

11

They were crammed into miserable, squalid slums, without proper sanitation, subjected to monstrous epidemics.

Instead of the development of civilisation bringing general happiness and well-being, it was giving rise to greater misery.

This was noted, not just by Marx, but by some of the other great thinkers of the period—men such as the English poets Blake and Shelley, the Frenchmen Fourier and Proudhon, the German philosophers Hegel and Feuerbach.

Hegel and Feuerbach called the unhappy state in which humanity found itself 'alienation'—a term you still often hear. By alienation, Hegel and Feuerbach meant that men and women continually found that they were dominated and oppressed by what they themselves had done in the past. So, Feuerbach pointed out, people had developed the idea of God—and then had bowed down before it, feeling miserable because they could not live up to something they themselves had made. The more society advanced, the more miserable, 'alienated', people became.

In his own earliest writings Marx took this notion of 'alienation' and applied it to the life of those who created the wealth of society.

'The worker becomes poorer the more wealth he produces, the more his production increases in power and range... With the increasing value of the world of things proceeds in direct proportion the devaluation of the world of men... The object which labour produces confronts it as something alien, as a power independent of the producer...'

In Marx's time the most popular explanations of what was wrong with society were still of a religious kind. The misery of society, it was said, was because of the failure of people to do what God wanted them to. If only we were all to 'renounce sin' everything would turn out all right.

A similar view is often heard today, although it usually purports to be non-religious. This is the claim that 'to change society, you must first change yourself'. If only individual men and women would cure themselves of

12

'selfishness' or 'materialism' (or occasionally 'hangups') then society would automatically get better.

A related view spoke not of changing *all* individuals, but a few key ones—those who exercise power in society. The idea was to try to make the rich and powerful 'see reason'.

One of the first British socialists, Robert Owen, began by trying to convince industrialists that they should be kinder to their workers. The same idea is still dominant today among the leaders of the Labour Party, including its left wing. Note how they always call the crimes of the employers 'mistakes', as if a bit of argument will persuade big business to relax its grip on society.

Marx referred to all such views as 'idealist'. Not because he was against people having 'ideas', but because such views see ideas as existing in isolation from the conditions in which people live.

People's ideas *are* intimately linked to the sort of lives they are able to live. Take, for instance, 'selfishness'. Present day capitalist society *breeds* selfishness—even in people who continually try to put other people first. A worker who wants to do their best for their children, or to give their parents something on top of their pension, finds the only way is to struggle continually against other people—to get a better job, more overtime, to be first in the queue for redundancy. In such a society you cannot get rid of 'selfishness' or 'greediness' merely by changing the minds of individuals.

It's even more ridiculous to talk of changing society by changing the ideas of 'top people'. Suppose you were successful in winning a big employer over to socialist ideas and he then stopped exploiting workers. He would just lose in competition with rival employers and be driven out of business.

Even for those who rule society what matters is not ideas, but the structure of the society in which they hold those ideas.

The point can be put another way. If ideas are what change society, where do the ideas come from? We live in a certain sort of society. The ideas put across by the press, the TV, the educational system and so on defend that sort of society. How has anyone ever been able to develop completely different ideas? Because their daily experiences contradict the official ideas of our society.

For example, you cannot explain why far fewer people are religious today than 100 years ago simply in terms of the success of atheistic propaganda. You have to explain why people *listen* to atheistic ideas in a way they did not 100 years ago.

Similarly, if you want to explain the impact of 'great men', you have to explain why other people agree to follow them. It is no good saying that, for example, Napoleon or Lenin changed history, without explaining why millions of people were willing to do what they suggested. After all, they were not mass hypnotists. Something in the life of society at a certain point led people to feel that what they suggested seemed correct.

You can only understand how ideas change history if you understand where those ideas come from and why people accept them. That means looking beyond the ideas to the *material* conditions of the society in which they occur. That is why Marx insisted: 'It is not consciousness that determines being, but social being that determines consciousness.'

2

Understanding history

IDEAS BY themselves cannot change society. This was one of Marx's first conclusions. Like a number of thinkers before him, he insisted that to understand society you had to see human beings as part of the material world.

Human behaviour was determined by material forces, just like the behaviour of any other natural object. The study of humanity was part of the scientific study of the natural world. Thinkers with such views were called *materialists*.

Marx regarded materialism as a great step forward over the various religious and idealist notions of history. It meant that you could argue *scientifically* about changing social conditions, you no longer depended on praying to God or on 'spiritual change' in people.

The replacement of idealism by materialism was the replacement of mysticism by science. But not all materialist explanations of human behaviour are correct. Just as there have been mistaken scientific theories in biology, chemistry or physics, so there have been mistaken attempts to develop scientific theories of society. Here are a few examples:

One very widespread, non-Marxist, materialist view holds that human beings are animals, who behave 'naturally' in certain ways. Just as it is in the nature of wolves to kill or in the nature of sheep to be placid, so it is in the nature of men to be aggressive, domineering, competitive and greedy (and, it is implied, of women to be meek, submissive, deferential and passive).

One formulation of this view is to be found in the best selling book *The Naked Ape*. The conclusions that are drawn from such arguments are almost invariably reactionary. If men are naturally aggressive, it is said, then there is no point in trying to improve society. Things will always turn out the same. Revolutions will 'always fail'.

But 'human nature' does in fact vary from society to society. For instance, competitiveness, which is taken for granted in our society, hardly existed in many previous societies. When scientists first tried to give Sioux Indians IQ tests, they found that the Indians could not understand why they should not help each other do the answers. The society they lived in stressed co-operation, not competition.

The same with aggressiveness. When Eskimos first met Europeans, they could not make any sense whatsoever of the notion of 'war'. The idea of one group of people trying to wipe out another group of people seemed to them crazy.

In our society it is regarded as 'natural' that parents should love and protect their children. Yet in the Ancient Greek city of Sparta it was regarded as 'natural' to leave infants out in the mountains to see if they could survive the cold.

'Unchanging human nature' theories provide no explanation for the great events of history. The pyramids of Egypt, the splendours of Ancient Greece, the empires of Rome or the Incas, the modern industrial city, are put on the same level as the illiterate peasants who lived in the mud hovels of the Dark Ages. All that matters is the 'naked ape'—not the magnificent civilisations the ape has built. It is irrelevant that some forms of society succeed in feeding the 'apes', while others leave millions to starve to death.

Many people accept a different materialist theory, which stresses the way it is possible to change human behaviour. Just as animals can be trained to behave differently in a circus to a jungle, so, say the supporters of this view, human behaviour can similarly be changed. If only the right people got control of society, it is said, then 'human nature' could be transformed.

16

This view is certainly a great step forward from the 'naked ape'. But as an explanation of how society as a whole can be changed it fails. If everyone is completely conditioned in present-day society, how can anyone ever rise above society and see how to change the conditioning mechanisms? Is there some God-ordained minority that is magically immune to the pressures that dominate everyone else? If we are all animals in the circus, who can be the lion tamer?

Those who hold this theory either end up saying society cannot change (like the Naked Apers) *or* they believe change is produced by something outside society—by God, or a 'great man', or the power of individual ideas. Their 'materialism' lets a new version of idealism in through the back door.

As Marx pointed out, this doctrine necessarily ends up by dividing society into two parts, one of which is superior to society. This 'materialist' view is often reactionary. One of the best known adherents of the view today is a right wing American psychologist called Skinner. He wants to condition people to behave in certain ways. But since he himself is a product of American capitalist society, his 'conditioning' merely means trying to make people conform to that society.

Another materialist view blames all the misery in the world on 'population pressure'. (This is usually called Malthusian after Malthus, the English economist of the late eighteenth century who first developed it.) But it cannot explain why the United States, for instance, burns corn while people in India starve. Nor can it explain why 150 years ago there was not enough food produced in the US to feed 10 million people, while today enough is produced to feed 200 million.

It forgets that every extra mouth to feed is also an extra person capable of working and creating wealth.

Marx called all these mistaken explanations forms of 'mechanical' or 'crude' materialism. They all forget that as well as being part of the material world, human beings are also acting, living creatures whose actions change it.

The materialist interpretation of history

'MEN CAN be distinguished from animals by consciousness, by religion or anything else you like. They themselves begin to distinguish themselves from animals as soon as they begin to *produce* their means of subsistence—their food, shelter and clothing'.

With these words, Karl Marx first stressed what was distinct about his explanation of how society developed. Human beings are animals descended from ape-like creatures. Like other animals, their first concern is feeding themselves and protecting themselves from the climate.

The way other animals do this depends on their inherited biological make-up. A wolf stays alive by chasing and killing its prey, in ways determined by its biologically inherited instincts. It keeps warm on cold nights because of its fur. It brings up its cubs according to inherited patterns of behaviour.

But human life is not fixed in this way. The humans who roamed the earth 100,000 years ago or 30,000 years ago lived quite different lives from ourselves. They lived in caves and holes in the ground. They did not have any containers to keep food or water in, they depended for their food on collecting berries or throwing stones at wild animals. They could not write, or count beyond the fingers on their hands. They had no real knowledge of what went on beyond their immediate neighbourhood or what their forefathers had done.

Yet physically their make-up 100,000 years ago was similar to that of modern man and 30,000 years ago it was identical. If you washed and shaved a caveman, put him in a suit and walked him down the High Street, no one would think him out of place.

As the archaeologist C Gordon Childe has noted: 'The earliest skeletons of our own species belong to the closing phases of the last Ice Age... Since the time when skeletons of homo sapiens first appear in the geological record... man's bodily evolution has come virtually to a standstill, although his cultural progress was just beginning.'

The same point is made by another archaeologist, Leakey: 'The physical differences between men of the Aurignacian and Magdalenian cultures (25,000 years ago) on the one hand, and present day men on the other is negligible, while the cultural difference is immeasurable'.

By 'culture' the archaeologist means the things which men and women learn and teach one another (how to make clothes from furs or wool, how to make pots out of clay, how to make fire, how to build homes, and so forth) as opposed to those things that animals know instinctively.

The lives of the earliest humans were already vastly different from those of other animals. For they were able to use the physical features peculiar to humans—large brains, forelimbs capable of manipulating objects—to begin to shape their surroundings to suit their needs. This meant humans could adapt themselves to a wide range of different conditions, without any change in their physical make-up. Humans no longer simply reacted to conditions around them. They could act upon those conditions, beginning to change them to their own advantage.

At first they used sticks and stones to attack wild beasts, they lit torches from naturally occurring fires to provide themselves with heat and light, they covered themselves with vegetation and animal skins. Over many tens of thousands of years they learnt to make fire themselves, to shape stones using other stones, eventually to grow food from seeds they themselves had planted, to store it in pots made out of clay, and to domesticate certain animals.

Comparatively recently—a mere 5,000 years ago, out of half a million years of human history—they learnt the secret of turning ores into metals that could be shaped into reliable tools and effective weapons.

Each of these advances had an enormous impact, not merely in making it easier for humans to feed and clothe themselves, but also in transforming the very organisation of human life itself. From the beginning human life was social. Only the joint efforts of several humans could enable them to kill the

19

beasts, to gather the food and keep the fires going. They had to co-operate.

This continual close co-operation also caused them to communicate, by uttering sounds and developing languages. At first the social groups were simple. There was not enough naturally growing produce anywhere to support groups of humans more than perhaps a couple of dozen strong. All effort had to be put into the basic tasks of getting the food, so everyone did the same job and lived the same sort of life.

With no means of storing any quantities of food, there could be no private property or class divisions, nor was there any booty to produce a motive for war.

There were, until a few years ago, still hundreds of societies in many different parts of the globe where this was still the pattern—among some of the Indians of North and South America, some of the peoples of Equatorial Africa and the Pacific Ocean, the Aborigines of Australia.

Not that these people were less clever than ourselves or had a more 'primitive mentality'. The Australian Aborigines, for instance, had to learn to recognise literally thousands of plants and the habits of scores of different animals in order to survive.

The anthropologist Professor Firth had described how:

'Australian tribes... know the habits, markings, breeding grounds and seasonal fluctuations of all the edible animals, fish and birds of their hunting grounds. They know the external and some of the less obvious properties of rocks, stones, waxes, gums, plants, fibres and barks; they know how to make fire; they know how to apply heat to relieve pain, stop bleeding and delay the putrefaction of fresh food; and they also use fire and heat to harden some woods and soften others... They know something at least of the phases of the moon, the movement of the tides, the planetary cycles, and the sequence and duration of the seasons; they have correlated together such climactic fluctuations as wind systems, annual patterns of humidity and temperature and fluxes in the growth and presence of natural species... In addition they make intelligent and economical use of the by-products of animals killed for food; the flesh of the kangaroo is eaten; the leg bones are used as fabricators for stone tools and as pins; the sinews become spear bindings; the claws are set into necklaces with wax and fibre; the fat is combined with red ochre as a cosmetic, and blood is mixed with charcoal as paint... They have some knowledge of simple mechanical principles and will trim a boomerang again and again to give it the correct curve...'

They were much more 'clever' than us in dealing with the problems of surviving in the Australian desert. What they had not learnt was to plant seeds and grow their own food—something our own ancestors learnt only about five thousand years ago, after being on the earth for a hundred times that period.

The development of new techniques of producing wealth—the means of human life—has always given birth to new forms of co-operation between humans, *to new social relations*.

For example, when people first learnt to grow their own food (by planting seeds and domesticating animals) and to store it (in earthenware pots) there was a complete revolution in social life—called by archaeologists 'the neolithic revolution'. Humans had to co-operate together now to clear the land and to harvest food, as well as to hunt animals. They could live together in much greater numbers than before, they could store food and they could begin to exchange goods with other settlements.

The first towns could develop. For the first time there was the possibility of some people leading lives that did not involve them just in providing food: some would specialise in making pots, some in mining flints and later metal for tools and weapons, some in carrying through elementary administrative tasks for the settlement as a whole. More ominously, the stored surplus of food provided a motive for war.

People had begun by discovering new ways of dealing with the world around them, or harnessing nature to their needs. But in the process, without intending it, they had transformed the society in which they lived and with it their own lives. Marx summed up this process: a development of the 'forces of

21

production' changed the 'relations of production' and, through them, society.

There are many, more recent examples.

Three hundred years ago the vast majority of people in this country still lived on the land, producing food by techniques that had not changed for centuries. Their mental horizon was bounded by the local village and their ideas very much influenced by the local church. The vast majority did not need to read and write, and never learned to.

Then, 200 years ago, industry began to develop. Tens of thousands of people were drawn into the factories. Their lives underwent a complete transformation. Now they lived in great towns, not small villages. They needed to learn skills undreamt of by their ancestors, including eventually the ability to read and write. Railways and steamships made it possible to travel across half the earth. The old ideas hammered into their heads by the priests no longer fitted at all. The material revolution in production was also a revolution in the way they lived and in the ideas they had.

Similar changes are still affecting vast numbers of people. Look at the way people from villages in Bangladesh or Turkey have been drawn to the factories of England or Germany seeking work. Look at the way many find that their old customs and religious attitudes no longer fit.

Or look at the way in the past 50 years the majority of women have got used to working outside the home and how this has led them to challenge the old attitudes that they were virtually the property of their husbands.

Changes in the way humans work together to produce the things that feed, clothe and shelter them cause changes in the way in which society is organised and the attitude of people in it. This is the secret of social change—of history—that the thinkers before Marx (and many since), the *idealists* and the *mechanical materialists*, could not understand.

The idealists saw there was change—but said it must come out of the skies. The mechanical materialists saw that humans were conditioned by the material world but could not understand how things could ever change. What Marx saw

22

was that human beings are conditioned by the world around them, but that they react back upon the world, working on it so as to make it more habitable. But in doing so they change the conditions under which they live and therefore themselves as well.

The key to understanding change in society lies in understanding how human beings cope with the problem of creating their food, shelter and clothing. That was Marx's starting point. But that does not mean that Marxists believe that improvements in technology *automatically* produce a better society, or even that inventions automatically lead to changes in society. Marx rejected this view (sometimes called technological determinism). Again and again in history, people have rejected ideas for advancing the production of food, shelter or clothing because these clash with the attitudes or the forms of society that already exist.

For example under the Roman Empire there were many ideas about how to produce more crops from a given amount of ground, but people didn't put them into effect because they required more devotion to work than you could get from slaves working under fear of the whip. When the British ruled Ireland in the eighteenth century they tried to *stop* the development of industry there because it clashed with the interests of businessmen in London.

If someone produced a method of solving the food problem of India by slaughtering the sacred cows or providing everyone in Britain with succulent steaks by processing rat meat, they would be ignored because of established prejudices.

Developments in production challenge old prejudices and old ways of organising society, but they do not automatically *overthrow* those old prejudices and social forms. Many human beings fight to prevent change—and those wanting to use new methods of production have to fight *for* change. If those who oppose change win, then the new forms of production cannot come into operation and production stagnates or even goes backwards.

In Marxist terminology: as the *forces of production* develop they clash with the pre-existing *social relations* and ideas

23

that grew up on the basis of old forces of production. Either people identified with the new forces of production win this clash, or those identified with the old system do. In the one case, society moves forward, in the other it remains stuck in a rut, or even goes backwards.

3

Class struggle

WE LIVE in a society that is divided into classes, in which a few people have vast amounts of private property, and most of us have virtually none. Naturally, we tend to take it for granted that things have always been like this. But in fact, for the greater part of human history, there were no classes, no private property, and no armies or police. This was the situation during the half a million years of human development up to 5,000 or 10,000 years ago.

Until more food could be produced by one person's work than was needed to keep that person fit for work, there *could* be no division into classes. What was the point of keeping slaves if all that they produced was needed to keep them alive?

But beyond a certain point, the advance of production made class divisions not only possible but necessary. Enough food could be produced to leave a *surplus* after the immediate producers had taken enough to stay alive. And the means existed to store this food and to transport it from one place to another.

The people whose labour produced all this food could simply have eaten the extra 'surplus' food. Since they lived fairly meagre, miserable lives, they were strongly tempted. But that left them unprotected against the ravages of nature, which might mean famine or a flood the next year, and against attacks from hungry tribes from outside the area.

It was, at first, of great advantage to everyone if a special group of people took charge of this extra wealth, storing

25

it against future disaster, using it to support craftsmen, building up means of defence, exchanging part of it with distant peoples for useful objects. These activities came to be carried out in the first towns, where administrators, merchants and craftsmen lived. Out of the markings on tablets used to keep a record of the different sorts of wealth, writing began to develop.

Such were the first, faltering steps of what we call 'civilisation'. But—and it was a very big but—all this was based on control of the increased wealth by a small minority of the population. And the minority used the wealth for its own good as well as the good of society as a whole.

The more production developed, the more wealth came into the hands of this minority—and the more it became cut off from the rest of society. Rules, which began as a means of benefiting society, became 'laws', insisting that the wealth and the land that produced it was the 'private property' of the minority. A *ruling class* had come into existence—and *laws* defended its power.

You might perhaps ask whether it would have been possible for society to have developed otherwise, for those who laboured on the land to control its produce?

The answer has to be No. Not because of 'human nature', but because society was still very poor. The majority of the earth's population were too busy scratching the soil for a meagre living to have time to develop systems of writing and reading, to create works of art, to build ships for trade, to plot the course of the stars, to discover the rudiments of mathematics, to work out when rivers would flood or how irrigation channels should be constructed. These things could only happen if some of the necessities of life were seized from the mass of the population and used to maintain a privileged minority which did not have to toil from sunrise to sunset.

However, that does not mean that the division into classes remains necessary today. The last century has seen a development of production undreamt of in the previous history of humanity. Natural scarcity has been overcome—what now exists is *artificial* scarcity, created as governments *destroy* food stocks.

26

Class society today is holding humanity back, not leading it forward.

It was not just the first change from purely agricultural societies to societies of towns and cities that gave rise, necessarily, to new class divisions. The same process was repeated every time new ways of producing wealth began to develop.

So, in Britain a thousand years ago, the ruling class was made up of feudal barons who controlled the land and lived off the backs of the serfs. But as trade began to develop on a big scale, there grew up alongside them in the cities a new privileged class of wealthy merchants. And when industry began to develop on a substantial scale, their power in turn was disputed by the owners of industrial enterprises.

At each stage in the development of society there was an oppressed class whose physical labour created the wealth, and a ruling class who controlled that wealth. But as society developed both the oppressed and the oppressors underwent changes.

In the *slave* society of Ancient Rome, the slaves were the personal property of the ruling class. The slave owner owned the goods produced by the slave because he owned the slave, in exactly the same way as he owned the milk produced by a cow because he owned the cow.

In the *feudal* society of the middle ages, the serfs had their own land, and owned what was produced from it; but in return for having this land they had to do a number of days' work every year on the land owned by the feudal lord. Their time would be divided: perhaps half their time they would be working for the lord, half the time for themselves. If they refused to do work for the lord, he was entitled to punish them (through flogging, imprisonment or worse).

In modern *capitalist* society, the boss does not physically own the worker nor is he entitled to physically punish a worker who refuses to do unpaid work for him. But the boss does own the factories where the worker has to get a job if he or she wants to keep alive. So it is fairly easy for him to force the worker to put up with a wage which is much less than the value of the goods the worker makes in the factory.

27

In each case the oppressing class gets control of all the wealth that is left over once the most elementary needs of the workers have been met. The slave owner wants to keep his property in a good condition, so he feeds his slave in exactly the same way as you might oil your car. But everything surplus to the physical needs of the slave, the owner uses for his own enjoyment. The feudal serf has to feed and clothe himself with the work he puts in on his own bit of land. All the extra labour he puts in on the lord's fields goes to the lord.

The modern worker gets paid a wage. All the other wealth he creates goes to the employing class as profit, interest or rent.

The class struggle and the state

THE WORKERS have rarely accepted their lot without fighting back. There were slave revolts in ancient Egypt and Rome, peasant revolts in Imperial China, civil wars between the rich and poor in the cities of Ancient Greece, in Rome and Renaissance Europe.

That is why Karl Marx began his pamphlet, *The Communist Manifesto*, by insisting that 'The history of all hitherto existing societies has been the history of class struggles'. The growth of civilisation had depended on the exploitation of one class by another, and therefore on the struggle between them.

However powerful an Egyptian pharoah, a Roman emperor or a mediaeval prince, however luxurious their lives, however magnificent their palaces, they could do nothing unless they guaranteed that the products grown by the most miserable peasant or slave passed into their possession. They could only do this if alongside the division into classes there also grew something else—control over the means of violence by themselves and their supporters.

In earlier societies there had been no army, police or governmental apparatus separate from the majority of the people. Even some 50 or 60 years ago, for instance, in parts of Africa, it was still possible to find societies in which this was still so. Many of the tasks done by the state in our society were simply done informally by the whole population, or by meetings of representatives.

Such meetings would judge the behaviour of any individual who was considered to have broken an important social rule. Punishment would be applied by the whole community—for instance by forcing miscreants to leave. Since everyone was agreed on the necessary punishment, separate police were not needed to put it into effect. If warfare occurred all the young men would take part, under leaders chosen for the occasion, again without any separate army structure.

But once you had a society in which a minority had control over most of the wealth, these simple ways of keeping 'law and order' and organising warfare could no longer work. Any meeting of representatives or any gathering of the armed young men would be likely to split along class lines.

The privileged group could only survive if it began to monopolise in its own hands the making and implementation of punishments, laws, the organisation of armies, the production of weapons. So the separation into classes was accompanied by the growth of groups of judges, policemen and secret policemen, generals, bureaucrats—all of whom were given part of the wealth in the hands of the privileged class in return for protecting its rule.

Those who served in the ranks of this 'state' were trained to obey without hesitation the orders of their 'superiors' and were cut off from all normal social ties with the exploited mass of people. The state developed as a killing machine in the hands of the privileged class. And a highly effective machine it could be.

Of course, the generals who ran this machine often fell out with a particular emperor or king, and tried to put themselves in his place. The ruling class, having armed a monster, could often not control it. But since the wealth needed to keep the killing machine running came from the exploitation of the working masses, every such revolt would be followed by continuation of society along the old lines.

Throughout history people who have really wanted to change society for the better have found themselves up against not just the privileged class, but also an armed machine, a state, that serves its interest.

Ruling classes, together with the priests, generals, policemen and legal systems that backed them up, all grew up in the first place because without them civilisation could not develop. But once they are established in power, they come to have an interest in hindering the further development of civilisation. Their power is dependent upon their ability to force those who produce wealth to hand it over to them. They become wary of new ways of producing wealth, even if more efficient than the old, lest control escape from their hands.

They fear anything that could lead to the exploited masses developing initiative and independence. And they also fear the growth of new privileged groups with enough wealth to be able to pay for arms and armies of their own. Beyond a certain point, instead of aiding the development of production, they began to hinder it.

For example, in the Chinese empire, the power of the ruling class rested upon its ownership of the land and its control over the canals and dams that were necessary for irrigation and to avoid floods. This control laid the basis for a civilisation that lasted some 2,000 years. But at the end of this period production was not much more advanced than at the beginning—despite the flourishing of Chinese art, the discovery of printing and gunpowder, all at a time when Europe was stuck in the Dark Ages.

The reason was that when new forms of production did begin to develop, it was in towns, through the initiative of merchants and craftsmen. The ruling class feared this growth in power of a social grouping that was not completely under its control. So periodically the imperial authorities took harsh measures to crush the growing economies of the towns, to drive production down, and to destroy the power of the new social classes.

The growth of new *forces of production*—of new ways of producing wealth—clashed with the interests of the old

30

ruling class. A struggle developed, the outcome of which determined the whole future of society.

Sometimes the outcome, as in China, was that new forms of production were prevented from emerging, and society remained more or less stagnant for very long periods of time.

Sometimes, as in the Roman empire, the inability of new forms of production to develop meant that eventually there was no longer enough wealth being produced to maintain society on its old basis. Civilisation collapsed, the cities were destroyed and people reverted to a crude, agricultural form of society.

Sometimes a new class, based upon a new form of production, was able to organise to weaken and finally overthrow the old ruling class, together with its legal system, its armies, its ideology, its religion. Then society could go forward.

In each case whether society went forwards or backwards depended on who won the war between the classes. And, as in any war, victory was not ordained in advance, but depended on the organisation, cohesion and leadership of the rival classes.

4

Capitalism— how the system began

ONE OF THE most ludicrous arguments you hear is that things could not be different to the way they are now. Yet things were different. And not on some distant part of the globe, but in this country, not so long ago. A mere 250 years ago people would have regarded you as a lunatic if you had described to them the world we live in now, with its huge cities, its great factories, its aeroplanes, its space expeditions, even its railway systems were beyond the bounds of their imagination.

For they lived in a society which was overwhelmingly rural, in which most people had never travelled ten miles outside their local village, in which the pattern of life was determined, as it had been for thousands of years, by the alternation of the seasons.

But already, seven or eight hundred years ago, a development had begun which was eventually to challenge this whole system of society. Groups of craftsmen and traders began to establish themselves in towns, not giving their services for nothing to some lord as the rest of the population did, but exchanging products with various lords and serfs for foodstuffs. Increasingly they used precious metals as a measure of that exchange. It was not a big step to seeing in every act of exchange an opportunity to get a little extra of the precious metal, to make a profit.

At first the towns could only survive by playing one lord off against another. But as the skills of their craftsmen improved, they created more wealth, and they grew in influence. The 'burgers', the 'bourgeois' or the 'middle classes' began as a class within the feudal society of the middle ages. But they obtained their riches in a quite different way to the feudal lords who dominated that society.

A feudal lord lived directly off the agricultural produce he was able to force his serfs to produce on his land. He used his personal power to make them do this, without having to pay them. By contrast the wealthier classes in the towns lived off the proceeds of selling non-agricultural goods. They paid workers wages to produce these for them, by the day or week.

These workers, often escaped serfs, were 'free' to come and go as they liked—once they had finished the work for which they had been paid. The 'only' compulsion on them to work was that they would starve if they did not find employment with someone. The rich could only grow richer because rather than starve, the 'free' worker would accept less money for his work than the goods he produced were worth.

We will return to this point later. For the present what matters is that the middle class burgers and the feudal lords got their wealth from quite different sources. This led them to want society organised in different ways.

The feudal lord's ideal was a society in which he had absolute power in his own lands, unbound by written laws, with no intrusion from any outside body, with his serfs unable to flee. He wanted things to stay as in the days of his father and grandfather, with everyone accepting the social station into which they were born.

The newly-rich bourgeois necessarily saw things differently. They wanted restraints on the power of individual lords or kings to interfere with their trade or steal their wealth. They dreamed of achieving this through a fixed body of written laws, to be drawn up and enforced by their own chosen representatives. They wanted to free the poorer classes from serfdom, so that they could work (and increase the burgers' profits) in the towns.

As for themselves, their fathers and grandfathers had often been under the thumb of feudal lords, and they certainly did not want that to continue.

In a word, they wanted to *revolutionise* society. Their clashes with the old order were not only economic, but also ideological and political. Ideological chiefly meant religious, in an illiterate society where the chief source of general ideas about society was church preaching.

Since the mediaeval church was run by bishops and abbots who were feudal lords in their own right, it propagated pro-feudal views, attacking as 'sinful' many of the practices of the urban bourgeoisie.

So in Germany, Holland, Britain and France in the sixteenth and seventeenth centuries the middle classes rallied to a religion of their own. Protestantism—a religious ideology that preached thrift, sobriety, hard work (especially for the workers!) and the independence of the middle class congregation from the power of bishops and abbots.

The middle class created a God in their image, in opposition to the God of the middle ages.

Today we are told at school or on television about the great religious wars and civil wars of that period as if they were just about religious differences, as if people were daft enough to fight and die merely because they disagreed over the role of the blood and body of Christ in the Holy Communion. But much more was at stake—the clash between two completely different forms of society, based upon two different ways of organising the production of wealth.

In Britain, the bourgeoisie won. Horrific as it must seem to our present ruling class, their ancestors consecrated their power by cutting off a king's head, justifying the act with the rantings of Old Testament prophets.

But elsewhere the first round went to feudalism. In France and Germany the Protestant bourgeois revolutionaries were wiped out after bitter civil wars (although a feudal version of Protestantism survived as the religion of northern Germany). The bourgeoisie had to wait two centuries and more before enjoying success, in the second round that began without religious clothing in 1789 in Paris.

Exploitation and surplus value

IN SLAVE and feudal societies the upper classes had to have legal controls over the mass of the working population. Otherwise those who worked for the feudal lord or the slave owner would have run away, leaving the privileged class with no-one to labour for it.

But the capitalist does not, usually, need such *legal* controls over the person of the worker. He doesn't need to own him or her, provided he ensures that the worker who refuses to work for the capitalist will starve. Instead of owning the worker, the capitalist can prosper providing he owns and controls the worker's source of livelihood—the machines and factories.

The material necessities of life are produced by the labour of human beings. But that labour is next to useless without tools to cultivate the land and to process naturally occurring materials. The tools can vary enormously—from simple agricultural implements such as ploughs and hoes to the complicated machines you find in modern automated factories. But without the tools even the most highly skilled worker is unable to produce the things needed for physical survival.

It is the development of these tools—usually referred to as 'the means of production'—that separates modern human beings from our distant ancestors of the Stone Age. Capitalism is based on the ownership of these means of production by a few people. In Britain today, for instance, one percent of the population owns 84 percent of the stocks and shares in industry. In their hands is concentrated effective control over the vast majority of the means of production—the machines, the factories, the oil fields, the best agricultural land. The mass of the population can only get a livelihood if the capitalists allow them to work at and with those means of production. This gives the capitalists immense power to exploit the labour of other people—even though in the eyes of the law 'all men are equal'.

It took some centuries for the capitalists to build up their monopoly control over the means of production. In this country, for instance, the parliaments of the seventeenth and eighteenth centuries had first to pass a succession of Enclosure Acts, which drove peasants away from their own means of production, the land which they had cultivated for centuries. The land became the property of a section of the capitalist class and the mass of the rural population were forced to sell their labour to capitalists or starve.

Once capitalism had achieved this monopoly of the means of production, it could afford to let the mass of the population enjoy apparent freedom and equality of political rights with the capitalists. For however 'free' the workers were, they still had to work for a living.

Pro-capitalist economists have a simple explanation of what then happens. They say that by paying wages the capitalist buys the labour of the worker. He must pay a fair price for it. Otherwise the worker will go and work for someone else. The capitalist gives a 'fair day's wage'. In return the worker should give a 'fair day's work'.

How then do they explain profit? This, they claim, is a 'reward' to the capitalist for his 'sacrifice' in allowing the means of production (his capital) to be put to use. It is an argument that can hardly convince any worker who gives it a moment's thought.

Take a company that announces a 'net rate of profit' of 10 percent. It is saying that if the cost of all the machinery, factories and so on that they own is £100 million, then they are left with £10 million profit after paying the wages, raw material costs and the cost of replacing the machinery that wears out in a year.

You don't have to be a genius to see that after ten years the company will have made a total profit of £100 million— the full cost of their original investment.

If it is 'sacrifice' that is being rewarded, then surely after the first ten years *all profits should cease*. For by then the capitalists have been paid back completely for the money they put in in the first place. In fact, however, the capitalist is twice as wealthy as before. He owns his original investment *and* the accumulated profits.

The workers, in the meantime, have sacrificed most of their life's energy to working eight hours a day, 48 weeks a year, in the factory. Are they twice as well off at the end of that time as at the beginning? You bet your boots they're not. Even if a worker saves assiduously, he or she won't be able to buy much more than a colour television set, a cheap central heating system or a second hand car. The worker will never raise the money to buy the factory he or she works in.

The 'fair day's work for a fair day's pay' has multiplied the capital of the capitalist, while leaving the worker with no capital and no choice but to go on working for roughly the same wage. The 'equal rights' of the capitalist and the worker have increased *inequality*.

One of Karl Marx's great discoveries was the explanation for this apparent anomaly. There is no mechanism that forces a capitalist to pay his workers the full value of the work they do. A worker employed, for example, in the engineering industry today might create £400 of new output a week. But that does not mean he or she will be paid this sum. In 99 cases out of 100, they will get paid considerably less.

The alternative they have to working is to go hungry (or live on the miserable sums handed out by the social security). So they demand not the full value of what they produce, but rather just enough to give them a more or less acceptable living standard. The worker is paid only enough to get him to put all his efforts, all his capacity for work (what Marx called his labour power) at the disposal of the capitalist each day.

From the capitalist's point of view, providing the workers are paid enough to keep them fit for work and to bring up their children as a new generation of workers, then they are being paid a fair amount for their labour power. But the amount of wealth needed to keep workers fit for work is considerably less than the amount of wealth they can produce once working—the value of their labour power is considerably less than the value created by their labour.

The difference goes into the pocket of the capitalist. Marx called it 'surplus value'.

The self expansion of capital

IF YOU read the writing of apologists for the present system, you will soon notice that they share a strange belief. Money, according to them, has a magical property. It can grow like a plant or animal.

When a capitalist puts his money in a bank he expects it to increase in amount. When he invests it in the shares of ICI or Unilever he expects to be rewarded by off-shoots of fresh money every year, in the form of dividend payments. Karl Marx noted this phenomenon, which he called the 'self expansion of capital', and set out to explain it. As we saw previously, his explanation began not with money, but with labour and the means of production. In present society, those with enough wealth can buy control of the means of production. They can then force everyone else to sell to them the labour needed to work the means of production. The secret of the 'self expansion of capital', of the miraculous capacity of money to grow for those who have plenty of it, lies in the buying and selling of this labour.

Let's take the example of a worker, who we'll call Jack, who gets a job with an employer, Sir Browning Browne. The work Jack can do in eight hours will create an additional amount of wealth—worth perhaps £48. But Jack will be willing to work for much less than this, since the alternative is social security. The efforts of pro-capitalist MPs such as the noxious Tory, Ian Sproat, ensure that he will only get £12 a day on social security to keep himself and his family. They explain that to give more would be to 'destroy the incentive to work'.

If Jack wants to get more than £12 a day he has to sell his ability to work, his labour power, even if he is offered much less than the £48 worth of wealth he can create in eight hours. He will be willing to work for, perhaps, the average wage, £28 a day. The difference, £20 a day, goes into the pocket of Sir Browning. It is Sir Browning's surplus value.

Because he had enough wealth to buy control of the means of production in the first place, Sir Browning Browne can guarantee growing richer by £20 a day for every worker he employs. His money keeps growing, his capital expanding, not because of some law of nature, but because his control of the means of production allows him to get someone else's labour on the cheap.

Of course, Sir Browning does not necessarily have all the £20 to himself, he may rent the factory or the land, he may have borrowed some of his initial wealth from other members of the ruling class. They demand in return a cut of the surplus value. So perhaps he forks out £10 to them as rent, interest and dividend payments, leaving himself with *only* £10 profit.

Those who live off dividends have probably never seen Jack in their lives. Nevertheless, it was not the mystical power of pound coins that gave them their income, but the all-too-physical sweat of Jack. The dividend, the interest payments and the profit all came out of the surplus value.

What decides how much Jack gets for his work? The employer will try to pay as little as possible. But in practice there are limits below which he cannot go. Some of these limits are physical—it is no good giving workers such miserable wages that they suffer from malnutrition and are unable to put any effort into their work. They also have to be able to travel to and from work, to have somewhere they can rest at night, so that they do not fall asleep over the machines.

From this point of view it is worth even paying for what the workers think of as 'little luxuries'—like a few pints in the evening, the television, the occasional holiday. These all make the worker more refreshed and capable of doing more work. They all serve to replenish his labour power. It is an important fact that where wages are 'held too low' the productivity of labour falls.

The capitalist has to worry about something else as well.

His firm will be in business for many years, long after the present set of workers have died out. The firm will require the labour of their children. So they have to pay the workers enough to bring up their children. They also have to ensure that the state provides these children with certain skills (such as reading and writing) through the educational system.

In practice, something else matters as well—what the worker *thinks* is a 'decent wage'. A worker who gets paid considerably less than this may well neglect his work, not worrying about losing his job since he thinks it is 'useless'.

All these elements that determine his wage have one thing in common. They all go towards making sure he has the life energy, the labour power, that the capitalist buys by the hour. The workers are paid the cost of keeping themselves and their families alive and fit for work.

In present capitalist society, one further point has to be noted. Huge amounts of wealth are spent on such things as police forces and weapons. These are used in the interests of the capitalist class by the state. In effect, they belong to the capitalist class, although they are run by the state. The value which is spent on them belongs to the capitalists, not the workers. It too is part of the surplus value.

Surplus value = profit + rent + interest + spending on the police, army and so on.

5

The labour theory of value

'BUT MACHINERY, capital, produces goods as well as labour. If so, it's only fair that capital as well as labour gets a share of the wealth produced. Every "factor of production" has to get its reward.'

That is how someone who has been taught a little pro-capitalist economics replies to the Marxist analysis of exploitation and surplus value. And at first sight the objection seems to make some sense. For, surely, you cannot produce goods without capital?

Marxists have never argued that you could. But our starting point is rather different. We begin by asking: where does capital come from? How did the means of production come into existence in the first place?

The answer is not difficult to find. Everything people have used historically to create wealth—whether a neolithic stone axe or a modern computer—once had to be made by human labour. Even if the axe was shaped with tools, the tools in turn were the product of previous labour.

That is why Karl Marx used to refer to the means of production as 'dead labour'. When businessmen boast of the capital they possess, in reality they are boasting that they have gained control of a vast pool of the labour of previous generations—and that does not mean the labour of *their* ancestors, who laboured no more than they do now.

The notion that labour was the source of wealth—usually referred to as the 'labour theory of value'—was not an original discovery of Marx. All the great pro-capitalist economists until his time accepted it.

Such men, like the Scottish economist Adam Smith or the English economist David Ricardo, were writing when the system of industrial capitalism was still fairly young—in the years just before and just after the French Revolution. The capitalists did not yet dominate and needed to know the real source of their wealth if they were ever to do so. Smith and Ricardo served their interests by telling them that labour created wealth, and that to build up their wealth they had to 'free' labour from the control of the old pre-capitalist rulers.

But it was not long before thinkers close to the working class began to turn the argument against the friends of Smith and Ricardo: if labour creates wealth, then labour creates capital. And the 'rights of capital' are no more than the rights of usurped labour.

Soon the economists who supported capital were pronouncing the labour theory of value to be a load of nonsense. But if you kick truth out the front door, it has a habit of creeping in the back.

Turn on the radio. Listen to it long enough and you will hear some pundit or other claim that what is wrong with the British economy is that 'people do not work hard enough', or another way of saying the same thing, 'productivity is too low'. Forget for a minute whether the argument is correct or not. Instead look closely at the way it is put. They never say 'machines do not work hard enough'. No, it is always *people*, the workers.

They claim that if only the workers worked harder, more wealth would be created, and that this would make possible more investment in new machinery. The people who use this argument may not know it, but they are saying that more work will create more capital. *Work, labour, is the source of wealth.*

42

Say I have a five pound note in my pocket. Why is that of use to me? After all, it's only a piece of printed paper. Its value to me lies in the fact that I can get, in exchange for it, something useful that has been made by someone else's labour. The five pound note, in fact, is nothing more than an entitlement to the products of so much labour. Two five pound notes are an entitlement to the products of twice as much labour, and so on.

When we measure wealth we are really measuring the labour that has been expended in creating it.

Of course, not everyone produces as much with their labour in a given time as everyone else. If I set out, for instance, to make a table, I might take five or six times as long as a skilled carpenter. But no one in their right mind would regard what I had made as five or six times as valuable as a table made by a skilled carpenter. They would estimate its value according to how much of the carpenter's labour would be needed to make it, not mine.

Say it would take a carpenter an hour to make a table, then they would say that the value of the table to them was the equivalent of one hour's labour. That would be the labour time *necessary* to make it, given the usual level of technique and skill in present society.

For this reason, Marx insisted that the measure of the value of something was not simply the time it took an individual to make it, but the time it would take an individual working with the average level of technology and the average level of skill—he called this average level of labour needed '*the socially necessary labour time*'. The point is important because under capitalism advances in technology are always taking place, which means that it takes less and less labour to produce goods.

For example, when radios were made with thermionic valves they were very expensive items, because it took a great deal of labour to make the valves, to wire them together and so on. Then the transistor was invented, which could be made and wired together with much less labour. Suddenly, all the

43

workers in the factories still making valve radios found that the value of what they were producing slumped. For the value of radios was no longer determined by the labour time needed to make them from valves, but instead by the time needed to make them with transistors.

One final point. Prices of some goods fluctuate wildly—on a day-to-day or a week-to-week basis. These changes can be caused by many other things besides changes in the amount of labour needed to make them.

When the frost in Brazil killed all the coffee plants the price of coffee shot up, because there was a shortage throughout the world and people were prepared to pay more. If tomorrow some natural catastrophe was to destroy all the televisions in Britain, there is no doubt the price of televisions would shoot up in the same way. What economists call 'supply and demand' continually causes such fluctuations in price.

For this reason, many pro-capitalist economists say that the labour theory of value is nonsense. They say that only supply and demand matter. But that is nonsense. For this argument forgets that when things fluctuate they usually fluctuate around an average level. The sea goes up and down because of tides, but that doesn't mean we cannot talk of a fixed point around which it moves, which we call 'sea level'.

Similarly, the fact that prices go up and down from day to day does not mean that there are not fixed values around which they fluctuate. For instance, if all the televisions were destroyed, the first new ones to be produced would be very much in demand and fetch a high price. But it would not be long before more and more were on the market, competing with each other until the price was forced down close to their value in terms of the labour time needed to make them.

Competition and accumulation

THERE WAS a time when capitalism did seem like a dynamic and progressive system. For most of human history, the lives of most men and women have been dominated by drudgery and exploitation. Industrial capitalism did not change this when it made its appearance in the eighteenth and nineteenth centuries.

But it did seem to put this drudgery and exploitation to some useful purpose. Instead of wasting vast amounts of wealth on luxury for a few parasitic aristocrats or in building luxury tombs for dead monarchs or in futile wars over which son of an emperor should rule some god-forsaken hole, it used wealth to build up the means of creating more wealth. The rise of capitalism was a period of growth in industry, cities, means of transportation, on a scale undreamt of in previous human history.

Strange as it may seem today, places such as Oldham and Halifax and Bingley were the home of miracles. Humanity had never before seen so much raw cotton and wool turned so quickly into cloth to clothe millions. This did not happen because of any special virtues possessed by the capitalists. They were always rather noxious people, obsessed only with getting wealth into their own hands by paying as little as possible for the labour they used.

Many previous ruling classes had been like them in this respect *without* building up industry. But the capitalists were different in two important respects.

The first we have dealt with—that they did not *own* workers, instead paying them by the hour for their ability to work, their labour power. They used wage-slaves, not slaves. Secondly, they did not themselves consume the goods their workers produced. The feudal landlord lived directly from the meat, bread, cheese and wine produced by his serfs. But the capitalist lived by selling to other people the goods produced by workers.

This gave the individual capitalist less freedom to behave as he pleased than the individual slave owner or feudal lord had. To sell goods, the capitalist had to produce them as cheaply as possible. The capitalist owned the factory and was all-powerful within it. But he could not use his power as he wished. He had to bow down before the demands of competition with other factories.

Let's go back to our favourite capitalist, Sir Browning Browne. Assume that a certain quantity of the cotton cloth produced in his factory took 10 hours of workers' time to turn out, but that some other factory could produce the same amount in five hours of workers' time. Sir Browning would not be able to charge the price for it equivalent to 10 hours of labour. No one in their right mind would pay this price when there was cheaper cloth just down the road.

Any capitalist who wanted to survive in business had to ensure that his workers worked as fast as possible. But that was not all. He also had to make sure that his workers were working with the most up to date machinery, so that their labour produced as many goods in an hour as did the labour of those working for other capitalists. The capitalist who wanted to stay in business had to make sure he owned ever greater amounts of means of production—or, as Marx put it, to accumulate capital!

The competition between capitalists produced a power, the market system, that had each and every one of them in its grip. It compelled them to speed up the work process all the time and to invest as much as they could afford in new machinery. And they could only afford the new machinery (and, of course, have their own luxuries on the side) if they kept workers' wages as low as they could.

Marx writes in his major work, *Capital*, that the capitalist is like a miser, obsessed with getting more and more wealth. But:

'What in the miser is mere idiosyncracy is, in the capitalist, the effect of a social mechanism in which he is but one of the wheels... The development of capitalist production makes it constantly necessary to keep increasing the amount of capital laid out in a given industrial undertaking, and competition makes the immanent laws of capitalist production to be felt by each individual capitalist as external coercive laws. It compels him to keep constantly extending his capital in order to preserve it. But extend it he cannot, except by means of progressive accumulation.

'Accumulate, accumulate! That is Moses and the prophets!'

Production does not take place to satisfy human need—even the human needs of the capitalist class—but in order to enable one capitalist to survive in competition with another capitalist. The workers employed by each capitalist find their lives dominated by the drive of their employers to accumulate faster than their rivals.

As Marx's *Communist Manifesto* put it: 'In bourgeois society living labour is but a means to accumulate dead labour... Capital is independent and has individuality, while the living person is dependent and has no individuality'.

The compulsive drive for capitalists to accumulate in competition with one another explains the great rush forward of industry in the early years of the system. But something else resulted as well—repeated economic crisis. Crisis is not new. It is as old as the system itself.

6

Economic crisis

'THE ACCUMULATION of wealth on the one hand, of poverty on the other'. That was how Marx summed up the trend of capitalism. Every capitalist fears competition from every other, so he works his employees as hard as possible, paying as low wages as he can get away with.

The result is a disproportion between the massive growth of means of production on the one hand, and the limited growth in wages and the number of workers employed on the other. This, Marx insisted, was the basic cause of economic crisis.

The easiest way to look at this is to ask: who buys the greatly expanding quantity of goods? The low wages of the workers mean they cannot afford the goods produced by their own labour. And the capitalists cannot increase wages, because that would be to destroy profit, the driving force of the system.

But if firms cannot sell the goods they produce, they have to shut down factories and sack workers. The total amount of wages then falls still more, and yet more firms cannot sell their goods. A 'crisis of overproduction' sets in, with goods piling up throughout the economy that people cannot afford to buy.

This has been a recurrent feature of capitalist society for the past 160 years.

But any quick witted apologist for the system will soon point out that there should be an easy way out of the crisis. All that's needed is that capitalists invest their profit in new factories and machines. That will provide jobs for workers, who in turn will then be able to buy the unsold goods. This means that as long as there's new investment all the goods produced can be sold and the system can provide full employment.

Marx was no fool and recognised this. Indeed, as we've seen, he realised that the competitive pressure on capitalists to invest was central to the system. But, he asked, does this mean the capitalists will invest all their profits, all the time?

The capitalist will only invest the goods if he thinks he is guaranteed a 'reasonable' profit.

If he doesn't think there is such a profit to be made, he won't risk his money in investment. He'll put it in the bank and leave it there.

Whether the capitalist invests or not depends on how he assesses the economic situation. When it looks right, the capitalists all rush to invest at the same time, falling over each other searching for construction sites, buying up machines, scouring the earth for raw materials, paying over the odds for skilled labour.

This is usually called the 'boom'.

But the frenzied competition for land, raw materials and skilled labour forces up the prices of these things. And suddenly a point is reached where some firms discover their costs have risen so much that all their profits have disappeared.

The investment boom all at once gives way to an investment 'slump'. No one wants new factories—construction workers are sacked. No one wants new machines—the machine tool industry goes into crisis. No one wants all the iron and steel that is being produced—the steel industry is suddenly working 'below capacity' and becomes 'unprofitable'. Closures and shutdowns spread from industry to industry, destroying jobs—and with them the ability of workers to buy the goods of other industries.

The history of capitalism is a history of such periodic lurches into crisis, into the insanity of unemployed workers going hungry outside empty factories, while stocks of 'unwanted' goods rot.

49

Capitalism creates these crises of overproduction *periodically*, because there is no planning, so there's no way to stop the stampede of capital into and out of investment all at once.

People used to think that the state could stop this. By intervening in the economy, increasing state investment when private investment was low, then reducing it when private investment caught up, the state would keep production on an even keel. But nowadays state investment too is part of the lunacy.

Look at British Steel. Some years ago, when the firm was still nationalised, steelworkers were told their jobs were being scrapped to make way for vast modern automatic furnaces designed to produce more steel more cheaply. Now they are being told that yet more workers must lose their jobs—because Britain was not the only country to embark on these massive investment plans. France, Germany, the United States, Brazil, Eastern Europe, even South Korea, all did the same. Now there's a world surplus of steel—a crisis of overproduction. State investment is being cut.

Steelworkers, of course, suffer both ways.

This is the price humanity is still paying for an economic system where the production of massive wealth is controlled by a small privileged group interested only in profit. It does not matter whether these small privileged groups own industry directly, or control it indirectly through their control of the state (as with British Steel). While they use this control to compete with each other for the largest share of the profits, whether nationally or internationally, it is the workers who suffer.

The final lunacy of the system is that the 'crisis of overproduction' is not overproduction at all. All that 'surplus' steel, for instance, could help solve world hunger. Peasants around the world have to plough the land with wooden ploughshares—steel ploughshares would increase food production. But the peasants have no money anyway, so the capitalist system isn't interested—there's no profit to be made.

Why crises tend to get worse

CRISES DO not just take place with monotonous regularity. Marx also predicted they would get worse as time went on.

Even if investment took place at an even rate, without fits and starts, it could not stop the overall trend towards crisis. This is because the competition between capitalists (and capitalist nations) forces them to invest in labour saving equipment.

In Britain today almost all new investments are designed to cut the number of workers employed. That is why there are *fewer* workers in British industry today than 10 years ago, even though output has increased over that time.

Only by 'rationalising production', by 'increasing productivity', and by cutting the workforce can one capitalist get a bigger share of the cake than another. But the result for the system as a whole is devastating. For it means that the number of workers does not increase at anything like the same speed as investment.

Yet it is the labour of workers that is the source of the profits, the fuel that keeps the system going. If you make bigger and bigger investments, without a corresponding increase in the source of profits, you are heading for a breakdown—just as surely as if you expected to drive a Jaguar on the amount of petrol needed to keep a Mini going.

That is why Marx argued 100 years ago that the very success of capitalism in piling up huge investments in new equipment led to a 'tendency of the rate of profit to decline' which means ever-worsening crises.

His argument can be applied very simply to capitalism today. Instead of the old picture of 'bad times' turning into 'good times', of slumps turning into booms, we seem to be in a never ending slump. Any spell of upturn, any drop in unemployment, is limited and short lived .

Apologists for the system say this is because investment is not high enough. Without new investment there are no new jobs, without new jobs there's no money to buy new goods. So far, we can agree with them—but we don't agree with their explanation why this is happening.

They blame wages. Wages are too high, they say, which cuts profits to the bone. Capitalists are frightened to invest because they won't get 'sufficient reward'.

But the crisis has continued through long years in which government pay policies have *cut* workers' living standards and pushed profits up. The years 1975-78 saw the biggest cut in workers' living standards this century, while the rich grew richer—the top 10 percent pushed up their share of the national cake from 57.8 percent in 1974 to 60 percent in 1976.

There still isn't enough investment to end the crisis—and that goes not just for Britain, but for other countries where wages have been cut back, for France, for Japan, for Germany.

We would do better to listen to what Karl Marx said 100 years ago than to listen to those who apologise for capitalism today.

Marx predicted that as capitalism got older, its crises would get worse because the source of profit, labour, does not increase nearly as rapidly as the investment needed to put labour to work. Marx wrote when the value of the plant and machinery needed to employ each worker was fairly low. It has shot up since then, until today it can be £20,000 or even £30,000. Competition between capitalist firms has forced them to use ever bigger and ever more expensive machinery. The point has been reached where, in most industries, it is taken for granted that new machinery means fewer workers.

The international economic agency, OECD, has predicted that employment in the world's major economies *will fall*, even if by some miracle investment soars.

Which it won't. Because capitalists care about their profit, and if their investment increases four-fold but their profit only doubles, they get really upset. Yet this is what must happen if industry grows more quickly than the source of profit, labour.

As Marx put it, the rate of profit will tend to fall. He predicted that a point would eventually be reached at which any new investment would seem a perilous venture. The scale of expenditure needed for new plant and machinery would be colossal, but the rate of profit would be lower than ever before. When this point was reached, each capitalist (or capitalist state) would fantasise about huge new investment programmes— but be afraid to make them for fear of going bust.

The world economy today is very much like that. Rover plans new production lines—but fears it will lose money. British Steel dreams of those big plants they planned—but have to keep them on ice because they cannot sell their present output. The Japanese shipbuilders have given up investing in new yards—and some of the old ones are being shut down.

The very success of capitalism in building ever vaster and more productive machinery has brought the system to the point of seemingly permanent crisis.

A point was reached in the slave societies of the ancient world and the feudal societies of the Middle Ages where either a revolution would transform society or it would enter a permanent crisis that would drive it backwards. In the case of Rome, the lack of a revolution led precisely to the destruction of Roman civilisation and to the Dark Ages. In the case of some feudal societies—Britain and, later, France—revolution destroyed the old order and enabled new social advance to take place, under capitalism.

Now capitalism itself faces the choice between permanent crisis, which eventually will plunge humanity back into barbarism through poverty and war, *or a socialist revolution.*

7

The working class

MARX BEGAN *The Communist Manifesto* with the statement, 'The history of all hitherto existing societies has been the history of class struggles.'

The question of how the ruling class was to force the oppressed class to keep producing wealth for it was crucial. Because of this, in every previous society, there had been enormous struggles between the classes which often culminated in civil war—the slave uprisings in Ancient Rome, the peasant uprisings in mediaeval Europe, the great civil wars and revolutions of the seventeenth and eighteenth centuries.

In all of these great struggles, the mass of the insurgent forces were from the most oppressed section of society. *But*, as Marx hastened to add, at the end of the day all their efforts served only to replace one privileged ruling minority with another. So, for example, in ancient China there were several successful peasant revolts—but they merely replaced one emperor with another. Similarly, those who made the greatest effort in the French revolution were the 'Bras Nus'—the poorer classes of Paris, but at the end of the day society was ruled not by them but by bankers and industrialists instead of the king and courtiers.

There were two main reasons for this failure of the lower classes to keep control of the revolutions in which they fought.

Firstly, the general level of wealth in society was fairly low. It was only because the vast mass of people were kept in abysmal poverty that a small minority had time and leisure to develop the arts and sciences to maintain civilisation. In other words, class division was necessary if society was to progress.

Secondly, the life of the oppressed classes did not prepare them to run society. By and large they were illiterate, they had little idea of what things were like outside their own immediate locality, and, above all, their everyday life divided each of them against the other. Each peasant was concerned with cultivating his own plot of land. Each craftsman in the town ran his own small business and was to some extent in competition with other craftsmen, not united with them.

Peasant revolts would start with vast numbers of people rising up to divide the land of the local feudal lords, but once the lord was defeated, they would fall to squabbling among themselves about how they would divide the land. As Marx put it, peasants were like 'potatoes in a sack'; they could be forced together by some outside power but were not capable of linking permanently to represent their own interests.

The workers who create the wealth under modern capitalism differ from all the previous lower classes. Firstly, the division of classes is no longer necessary for human progress. So much wealth is created that capitalist society itself periodically destroys huge quantities through wars or economic crises. It could be divided up equally and society could still have a flowering of science, arts and so forth.

Secondly, life under capitalism prepares workers in many ways to take control of society. For example, capitalism needs workers who are skilled and educated. Also capitalism forces thousands of people into huge workplaces in huge conurbations where they are in close contact with one another, and where they can be a powerful force for changing society.

Capitalism makes workers cooperate in production within the factory, and those cooperative skills can easily be turned against the system, as when workers organise themselves into unions. Because they are massed together in huge concentrations it is much easier for workers to democratically control such bodies than it was for previously oppressed classes.

Furthermore, capitalism tends increasingly to turn groups

55

of people who thought of themselves as a 'cut above' ordinary workers (such as clerks or technicians) into wage labourers who are forced to organise unions and so on as other workers do.

Lastly, the development of communications—railways, roads, air transport, postal systems, telephones, radio and television—allows workers to communicate outside their own locality or industry. They can organise as a class on a national and international scale—something beyond the wildest dreams of previous oppressed classes.

All these facts mean that the working class can not only be a force which rebels against existing society, but can organise itself, electing and controlling its own representatives, so as to change society in its own interest, and not just to set up yet another emperor or group of bankers. As Karl Marx put it:

'All previous historical movements were movements of minorities in the interests of minorities. The proletarian movement is the self conscious independent movement of the immense majority in the interests of the immense majority.'

8

How can society be changed?

IN BRITAIN the overwhelming majority of socialists and trade unionists have generally argued that society can be transformed *without* violent revolution. All that is needed, they say, is for socialists to win enough popular support to gain control of the 'traditional' political institutions—parliament and the local councils. Then socialists will be in a position to change society by getting the existing state—the civil service, the judiciary, the police, the armed forces—to enforce laws to curtail the power of the employing class.

In this way, it has been claimed, socialism can be introduced *gradually* and without violence, by reforming the present set-up.

This view is usually referred to as 'reformism', although occasionally you will hear it referred to as 'revisionism' (because it involves revising Marx's ideas completely), 'social democracy' (although until 1914 that meant revolutionary socialism) or Fabianism (after the Fabian Society who have long propagated the reformist view in Britain). It is a view accepted by the left as well as the right of the Labour Party.

Reformism seems, at first sight, very plausible. It fits with what we are told at school, in the papers and on TV—that 'parliament runs the country' and that 'parliament is elected according to the democratic wishes of the people'. Yet despite that, every attempt to introduce socialism through parliament has ended in failure. Thus there have been three majority Labour governments in Britain since the war—with massive majorities in 1945 and 1966—yet we are no nearer socialism than in 1945.

The experience abroad is the same. In Chile in 1970, the socialist Salvador Allende was elected president. People claimed that this was a 'new way' to move to socialism. Three years later the generals who had been asked to join the government overthrew Allende and the Chilean working class movement was destroyed.

There are three inter-connected reasons why reformism must always fail.

Firstly, while socialist majorities in parliaments are 'gradually' introducing socialist measures, real *economic* power continues to lie in the hands of the old ruling class. They can use this economic power to shut down whole sections of industry, to create unemployment, to force up prices through speculation and hoarding, to send money abroad so creating a 'balance of payments' crisis, and to launch press campaigns blaming all this on the socialist government.

Thus Harold Wilson's Labour government was forced in 1964 and again in 1966 to drop measures which would have benefited the workers—by the wholesale movement of money abroad by wealthy individuals and companies. Wilson himself describes in his memoirs how: 'We had now reached the situation where a newly elected government was being told by international speculators that the policy on which we had fought the election could not be implemented... The Queen's first minister was being asked to bring down the curtain on parliamentary democracy by accepting the doctrine that an election in Britain was a farce, that the British people could not make a choice between policies.'

It only needs to be added that despite Wilson's alleged indignation, for the next six years he did indeed follow the sort of policies demanded by the speculators.

The same deliberate creation of balance of payments

crises forced the Labour government elected in 1974 to introduce three consecutive sets of cuts in public spending in hospitals, schools and social services.

Allende's government in Chile faced even greater disruption at the hands of big business. Twice, whole sections of industry were shut down by 'bosses' strikes', as speculation increased prices to an enormous level and hoarding of goods by businessmen caused queuing for the necessities of life.

The second reason capitalism cannot be reformed is that the existing state machine is not 'neutral', but designed, from top to bottom, to preserve capitalist society.

The state controls nearly all the means of exercising physical force, the means of violence. If the organisations of the state were neutral, and did whatever any particular government told them, whether capitalist or socialist, then the state could be used to stop sabotage of the economy by big business. But look at the way the state machine operates and who really gives the orders, and you can see it is not neutral.

The state machine is not simply the government. It is a vast organisation with many different branches—the police, the army, the judiciary, the civil service, the people who run the nationalised industries and so on. Many of the people who work in these different branches of the state come from the working class—they live and get paid like workers.

But it is not these people who make the decisions. The rank and file soldiers don't decide where wars are going to be fought or whether strikes are going to be broken; the counter clerk in the social security office does not decide how much dole will be paid out. The whole state machine is based on the principle that people on one rung on the ladder obey those on the rung above.

This is essentially the case in the sections of the state machine that exercise physical force—army, navy, airforce, police. The first thing soldiers are taught when they enlist—long before they are allowed to touch weapons—is to obey orders, regardless of their personal opinions of those orders. That is why they are taught to do absurd drills. If they will follow lunatic commands on the parade ground without thinking about it, it is reckoned they will shoot when ordered to without thinking about that either.

The most heinous crime in any army is a refusal to obey orders—mutiny. So seriously is the offence regarded, that mutiny during time of war is still punishable by execution in Britain.

Who gives the orders?

If you look at the chain of command in the British army (and other armies are no different) it goes General—Brigadier—Colonel—Lieutenant—NCO—Private. At no stage in that chain of command do elected representatives—MPs or local councillors—get a look in. It is just as much an act of mutiny for a group of privates to obey their local MP rather than the officer.

The army is a massive *killing machine*. The people who run it—and have the power to promote other soldiers into commanding positions—are the generals.

Of course, in theory the generals are responsible to the elected government. But soldiers are trained to obey generals, not politicians. If generals choose to give orders to their soldiers which are at variance with the wishes of an elected government, the government cannot countermand those orders. It can only try to persuade the generals to change their minds. *If* the government knows the sorts of orders that are being given—because military affairs are invariably secret, it is very easy for generals to hide what they are doing from governments they don't like.

That doesn't always mean that generals always, or even usually, ignore what governments say to them. Usually in Britain they have found it convenient to go along with most of what the government suggests. But, in a life and death situation, the generals are able to put their killing machine into operation without listening at all to the government, and there is little the government can do about it. This is what the generals eventually did in Chile when Allende was overthrown .

So the question '*Who runs the army?*' is really '*Who are the generals?*' In Britain about 80 percent of the senior officers went to fee-paying, 'public' schools—the same proportion as 50 years ago (a total of 17 years of Labour government hasn't changed *that*). They are related to the owners of big business, belong to the same posh clubs, mix at the same social functions, share the same ideas (if you doubt this, look at the letters column in virtually any copy of the *Daily Telegraph*). The same goes for the heads of the civil service, the judges, the chief constables.

Do you think these people are going to obey government orders to take economic power away from their friends and relatives in big business, just because 330 people walk into a lobby in the House of Commons? Would they not be much more likely to copy the example of the Chilean generals, judges and senior civil servants, who sabotaged the government's orders for three years and then, when the time was ripe, overthrew it?

In practice the particular 'constitution' we have in Britain means that those who control the state machine would be able to thwart the will of an elected left wing government far short of physically overthrowing it. If such a government were elected, it would be faced with massive economic sabotage by the employing class (factory closures, flights of money abroad, hoarding of necessities, inflationary price rises). If the government attempted to deal with such sabotage using 'constitutional means'—by passing laws—it would find its hands tied behind its back.

The House of Lords would certainly refuse to ratify any such law—delaying it for nine months at a minimum. The judges would 'interpret' any law passed in such a way as to curtail its powers. The civil service chiefs, the generals and the police chiefs would use the decisions of the judges and the House of Lords to justify their own unwillingness to do what ministers told them. They would be backed by virtually the whole press, which would scream that the government was behaving 'illegally' and 'unconstitutionally'. The generals would then use such language to justify preparations to overthrow an 'illegal' government.

The government would be *powerless* to deal with the

economic chaos—unless it really did act unconstitutionally and called upon rank and file civil servants, police and soldiers to turn against their superiors.

Lest anyone thinks this is all wild fantasy, it should be added that there have been at least two occasions in recent British history when generals *have* sabotaged government decisions they did not like.

In 1912 the House of Commons passed a Bill providing for a 'home rule' parliament to run a *united* Ireland. The Tory leader, Bonar Law, immediately denounced the (Liberal!) government as an illegal 'junta' who had 'sold the constitution'. The House of Lords naturally delayed the law as long as it could (two years then), while former Tory minister, Edward Carson, organised a paramilitary force in the north of Ireland to resist the law.

When the generals who commanded the British army in Ireland were told to move their troops northwards to deal with this force, they refused and threatened to resign their commissions. It was because of this action, usually called the 'Curragh Mutiny', that Ireland north and south didn't get a single parliament in 1914, and remains a divided nation even today.

In 1974 there was a rerun of the events of 1912 in miniature. The right wing sectarian Loyalists of Northern Ireland organised a general stoppage of industry, using barricades to prevent people going to work, against being forced to accept a joint Protestant-Catholic government in Northern Ireland. British ministers called on the British army and the Northern Ireland police, the Royal Ulster Constabulary, to dismantle the barricades and end the strike. The senior army officers and the police commanders told the government that this would be inadvisable, and neither soldiers nor police moved against the Loyalists. The joint Protestant-Catholic government was forced to resign, the views of army officers proving more powerful than the views of the British government.

If that could happen in 1914 and 1974 with middle-of-the-road governments trying to push through mild measures, imagine what would happen if a militant socialist government was elected. Any *serious* reformist majority in parliament would soon be forced to make a choice: either abandon reforms in order to placate those who own industry and control the key positions in the state, or prepare for an all-out conflict, which will inevitably mean the use of some kind of force, against those who control those positions.

The third reason why reformism is a dead end is that parliamentary 'democracy' contains inbuilt mechanisms for preventing any revolutionary movement finding expression through it.

Some reformists argue that the best way to take on the power of those who control the key positions in the state machine is for the left to obtain a majority in parliament first. This argument falls because parliaments always understate the level of revolutionary consciousness of the mass of the population.

The mass of the people will only believe that they themselves can run society when they begin in practice to change society through struggle. It is when millions of people are occupying their factories or taking part in a general strike that ideas of revolutionary socialism suddenly seem realistic.

But such a level of struggle cannot be maintained indefinitely unless the old ruling class is removed from power. If it hangs on, it will wait until the occupations or strikes decline, then use its control over the army and police to break the struggle.

And once the strikes or occupations begin to falter, the feeling of unity and confidence among the workers begins to wane. Demoralisation and bitterness set in. Even the best begin to feel that changing society was just a wild dream.

That is why employers *always* prefer strike votes to be taken when workers are at home by themselves, getting their ideas from the TV and the newspapers, not when they are united at mass meetings, able to hear other workers' arguments.

That is also why anti union laws nearly always include a clause *forcing* workers to call off strikes while secret, postal ballots are taken. Such clauses are accurately called 'cooling off' periods—they are designed to pour cold water on the confidence and unity of workers.

The parliamentary electoral system contains *built in* secret ballots and cooling off periods. For instance, if a government is brought to its knees by a massive strike, it is likely to say: 'OK, wait three weeks until a general election can resolve the question democratically.' It hopes that in the interim the strike will be called off. The workers' confidence and unity will then fade. Employers may well be able to blacklist militants. The capitalist press and the TV can begin functioning normally again, hammering home pro-government ideas. The police can arrest 'troublemakers'.

Then when the election finally takes place, the vote will not reflect the high point of the workers' struggles, but the low point after the strike.

In France in 1968, the government of General de Gaulle used elections in precisely this way. The reformist workers' parties and unions told workers to end their strikes, and de Gaulle won the election.

The British prime minister Edward Heath tried the same trick when faced with a massively successful miners' strike in 1974. But this time the miners were not conned. They kept their strike up—and Heath lost the election.

If workers wait for elections to decide the key issues in the class struggle, they will never reach that high point.

The workers' state

MARX IN his pamphlet *The Civil War in France*, and Lenin in *The State and Revolution* outlined a completely different view of how socialism can be won. Neither simply pulled these ideas out of thin air: both developed their views by seeing the working class in action—Marx saw the Paris Commune, Lenin the Russian 'soviets' (workers' councils) of 1905 and 1917.

But Marx and Lenin insisted that the working class could not begin to construct socialism until it had first destroyed the old state based on bureaucratic chains of command, and secondly created a new state based on entirely new principles. Lenin underlined how completely different this state had to be from the old by calling it 'a commune state, a state-which-is-not-a-state'.

A new state, Marx and Lenin said, was necessary if the working class was to impose its dictates on the remnants of the old ruling and middle classes. That was why they called it the 'dictatorship of the proletariat'—the working class had *to dictate* how society was to be run. It also had to defend its revolution against attacks from ruling classes elsewhere in the world. To do these two jobs, it had to have armed forces of its own, some form of policing of society, courts, even prisons.

But if this new army, police and legal system was to be controlled by the workers, and never turn against their interests, it had to be based on completely different principles from the capitalist state. It had to be the means by which the working class as a majority dictated to the rest of society, *not* a dictatorship directed against the majority of the working class.

The main differences are these.

The capitalist state serves the interests of a small minority of society. The workers' state has to serve the interests of the overwhelming majority. *Force* in the capitalist state is exercised by a minority of hired killers, cut off from the rest of society and trained to obey upper class officers. But in a workers' state, force would be needed only so the majority could protect themselves against anti social acts by the remnants of the old privileged classes.

Soldiering and policing in a workers' state can be done by ordinary workers, who mix freely with their fellow workers, share the same ideas and lead the same lives. Indeed, to make sure that groups of soldiers and police never develop separated from the mass of workers, the 'soldiers' and 'police' should be ordinary factory and office workers who take it in turns, on a rota system, to carry out these functions.

Instead of the armed forces and police being run by a small group of officers, they would be run by directly elected representatives of the mass of workers.

Parliamentary representatives in a capitalist state pass

laws, but leave it to full time bureaucrats, police chiefs and judges to implement them. This means that MPs and councillors can always hide behind a million excuses when their promises are not implemented. The workers' representatives in a workers' state would have to see their laws put into action. They, not an elite of top bureaucrats, would have to explain to the workers of the civil service, the army and so on how things should be done. Again elected workers' representatives would have to interpret the laws in courts.

Parliamentary representatives in a capitalist state are cut off from those who elect them by high salaries. In a workers' state the representatives would get no more than the average workers' wage. The same goes for those who work full time in key posts implementing the decisions of the workers' representatives (the equivalent of present-day civil servants).

Workers' representatives, and all those concerned with implementing workers' decisions, would not be as MPs, immune to removal from office for five years (or for life in the case of senior civil servants). They would be subject to at least annual elections, and to immediate recall by those who elected them if they did not implement their wishes.

Parliamentary representatives are elected by all the people living in a certain locality—upper class, middle class and working class, slum landlords as well as tenants, stockbrokers as well as labourers. In a workers' state election would be by those who work only, with voting only after open discussion on the issues concerned. So the core of the workers' state would be workers' councils based on the factories, mines, docks, big offices, with groups such as housewives, pensioners, school students and students having their own representatives.

In this way, each section of the working class would have its own representative and be able directly to judge whether he or she was following their interests. In these ways, the new state cannot become a force separate from and against the majority working class—as it was in Eastern bloc countries which called themselves Communist.

At the same time, the workers' council system provides a means by which workers can coordinate their efforts in running industry according to a democratically decided national plan, and not end up running their factories in competition with each other. It is easy to see how modern computer technology would enable all workers to be given information on the various economic options open to society, and to direct their representatives to choose what the majority of workers thought the best set of options—for example, whether to spend resources on Concorde or on a cheap and reliable public transport system, whether to build nuclear bombs or kidney machines, and so on.

The withering away of the state

BECAUSE STATE power would not be something *separate* from the mass of the workers, it would be much less a matter of coercion than under capitalism. As the remnants of the old society against which it was directed became resigned to the success of the revolution, and as revolutions removed foreign ruling classes, there would be less and less need for coercion, until eventually workers need never take time off from work to staff the 'police' and the 'army'.

This is what Marx and Lenin meant when they said the state would *wither away*. Instead of coercion against people, the state would become merely a mechanism of workers' councils to decide how to produce and allocate goods.

Workers' councils have come into being in one form or another whenever the struggle between the classes within capitalism has reached a really high level. 'Soviet' is the word the Russians used for 'workers' councils' in 1905 and 1917.

In 1918 in Germany workers' councils were, briefly, the only power in the country. In Spain in 1936 the various workers' parties and unions were united by 'militia committees' which ran the localities and were very much like workers' councils. In Hungary in 1956 the workers elected councils to run the factories and the localities as they fought Russian troops. In Chile in 1972-73 the workers began to build 'cordones'—workers' committees that linked the big factories.

The workers' council begins life as a body workers use to coordinate their struggle against capitalism. It may start with modest functions, raising strike funds maybe, but because these bodies are based on direct election from the workers, with workers' representatives subject to recall, they can at the highest points in the struggle coordinate the efforts of the whole working class. They can lay the basis for workers' power.

9

How do workers become revolutionary?

IN BRITAIN most workers this century have looked to the Labour Party and parliament to change society. A large minority have backed the reactionary ideas of the Tory Party. The supporters of revolutionary socialism have generally been few in number.

This indifference or even opposition of workers to revolutionary socialism is hardly surprising. We have all been brought up in a capitalist society where it is taken for granted that everyone is selfish, where people are continually told by the newspapers and TV that only a privileged minority have the ability to take the key decisions in industry and the state, where the mass of workers are taught from the first day they enter school to obey orders given by 'their elders and betters'.

As Marx put it, 'the ruling ideas are the ideas of the ruling class' and vast numbers of workers accept them.

Yet despite this, repeatedly in the history of capitalism, revolutionary movements of the working class have shaken one country after another: France in 1871, Russia in 1917, Germany and Hungary in 1919, Italy in 1920, Spain and France in 1936, Hungary in 1956, France in 1968, Chile in 1972-3, Portugal in 1975, Iran in 1979.

The explanation for these upheavals lies in the very nature of capitalism itself. Capitalism is a crisis-prone system. In the long run it cannot provide full employment, it cannot provide prosperity for all, it cannot secure our living standards today against the crisis it will produce tomorrow. But during the capitalist 'booms' workers come to expect these things.

So, for instance, in the 1950s and early 1960s, workers in Britain came to expect permanent full employment, a 'welfare state' and gradual but real improvements in living standards. By contrast, over the past two decades successive governments have allowed unemployment to increase to a real figure of 4 million, have cut the welfare state to shreds, and have attempted again and again to cut living standards.

Because we are brainwashed into accepting many capitalist ideas, we accept some of these attacks. But inevitably a point is reached where workers find they can stand it no more. Suddenly, often when no one expects it, their anger suddenly flares and they take some action against employer or government. Perhaps they stage a strike, or organise a demonstration.

When this happens, whether they like it or not, workers begin doing things that contradict all the capitalist ideas they have previously accepted. They begin to act in solidarity with one another, as a class, in opposition to the representatives of the capitalist class.

The ideas of revolutionary socialism that they used to reject out of hand now begin to fit in with what they are doing. Some at least of the workers begin to take those ideas seriously—providing those ideas are accessible.

The scale on which this takes place depends on the scale of the struggle, *not* on the ideas in workers' heads to begin with. Capitalism forces them into struggle even if they begin with pro-capitalist ideas. The struggle then makes them question these ideas.

Capitalist power rests on two planks—control of the means of production and control of the state. A real revolutionary movement begins among the vast mass of workers when struggles over their immediate economic interests lead them to clash with both planks of capitalist rule.

Take for example a group of workers who have been employed in the same factory for years. The whole normal humdrum pattern of their lives is dependent on their jobs there. One day the employer announces that he is going to close the factory down. Even the Tory voters in the workforce are horrified and want to do something. In desperation they decide that the only way to continue to lead the sort of lives capitalism has taught them to expect is to occupy the factory—to challenge the employer's control over the means of production.

They may soon find themselves up against the state as well, as the employer calls in the police to return control of 'his' property back to him. If they are to have any chance of keeping their jobs, the workers now must also confront the police, the state machine, as well as the employer.

Thus capitalism itself creates the conditions of class conflict which open workers' minds to ideas quite opposed to those which the system has taught them. This explains why the history of capitalism has been marked by periodic upsurges of revolutionary feeling among millions of workers, even if most of the time most workers accept the ideas the system feeds them.

One final point. One of the biggest things holding many workers back from support for revolutionary ideas is the feeling that it is not worth them personally doing anything because other workers will never support them. When they find that other workers are doing things, they suddenly lose their own apathy. In the same way people who feel that they, as workers, are quite incapable of running society do suddenly learn otherwise when they find, in the course of massive struggles against existing society, that they're taking over much of its running.

It is because of this that once revolutionary movements start, they can snowball at amazing speed.

10

The revolutionary socialist party

THE BASIC PREMISE of Marxism is that the development of capitalism itself drives workers into revolt against the system.

When such revolts break out—whether a mass demonstration, an armed insurrection or even a big strike—the transformation of working class consciousness is astonishing. All the mental energy that workers previously frittered away on a hundred and one diversions—from doing the horses to watching the telly—is suddenly directed towards trying to deal with the problem of how to change society. Millions of people working on such problems produce solutions of amazing ingenuity, which often leave established revolutionaries as bewildered as the ruling class by this turn of events.

So, for instance, in the first Russian revolution of 1905 a new form of workers' organisation, the Soviet—the workers' council—grew out of the strike committee set up during a printing strike. At first the Bolshevik Party—the most militant of the revolutionary socialists—treated the Soviets with distrust: they did not believe it was possible for the mass of previously non-political workers to create a genuinely revolutionary instrument.

Such experiences are found in many strikes: the established militants are taken completely by surprise when workers who have ignored their advice for so long, suddenly begin to organise militant action themselves.

This *spontaneity* is fundamental. But it is wrong to draw the conclusion—as anarchists and near-anarchists do—that because of spontaneity, there is no need for a revolutionary party.

In a revolutionary situation, millions of workers change their ideas very, very quickly. But they do not all change all their ideas at once. Inside every strike, every demonstration, every armed uprising there are always continual arguments. A few workers will see the action they are taking as a prelude to the working class taking control of society. Others will be half against taking any action at all, because it is disturbing the 'natural order of things'. In the middle will be the mass of workers, attracted first by one set of arguments, then by the other.

Onto one side of the balance the present ruling class will throw all the weight of its newspaper propaganda machine, denouncing the workers' actions. It will throw too its strike breaking forces, whether police, army or right wing organisations.

And on the workers' side of the argument there must be an organisation of socialists who can draw on the lessons of past class struggle, who can throw the arguments about socialism onto the balance. There must be an organisation that can draw together the growing understanding of workers in struggle, so they can act together to change society.

And this revolutionary socialist party needs to be there *before* the struggle starts, for organisation is not born spontaneously. The party is built through the continual interplay of socialist ideas and experience of the class struggle—for merely to *understand* society is not enough: only by applying these ideas in the day-to-day class struggle, in strikes, demonstrations, campaigns, will workers become aware of their power to change things, and gain the confidence to do it.

At certain points, the intervention of a socialist party can be decisive, can tip the balance towards change, towards a revolutionary transfer of power to the workers, towards a socialist society.

What sort of party?

THE REVOLUTIONARY socialist party needs to be *democratic*. To fulfil its role, the party must be continually in touch with the class struggle, and that means with its own members and supporters in the workplaces where that struggle takes place. It needs to be democratic because its leadership must always reflect the collective experience of the struggle.

At the same time, this democracy is not merely a system of election, but a continual debate within the party—a continual interaction of the socialist ideas on which the party is based with the experience of class struggle.

But the revolutionary socialist party must also be *centralised*. For it is an active party, not a debating society. It needs to be able to intervene collectively in the class struggle, and to respond quickly, so it must have a leadership capable of taking day-to-day decisions in the name of the party.

If the government orders the jailing of pickets, for instance, the party needs to react at once, without the need to convene conferences to take democratic decisions first. So the decision is made centrally and acted upon. Democracy comes into play afterwards, when the party hammers out whether the decision was correct or not—and maybe changes the party leadership if it was out of touch with the needs of the struggle.

The revolutionary socialist party needs to maintain a fine and delicate balance between democracy and centralism. The key is that the party does not exist for its own sake, but as a means for bringing a revolutionary change to socialism— and that can only be through *class* struggle.

So the party must continually adapt itself to the struggle. When the struggle is low, and few workers believe in the possibility of revolutionary change, then the party will be small—and must be content to be so for to dilute its political

74

ideas in order to increase its membership would be pointless. But when the struggle increases, large numbers of workers can change their ideas very fast, realising through struggle their power to change things—and then the party must be able to open its doors, otherwise it will be left on the sidelines.

The party cannot *substitute* for the working class. It must be *part* of the class struggle, continually trying to unite the most class conscious workers to provide a leadership for the struggle. Nor can the party dictate to the class. It cannot simply proclaim itself the leadership, but must win that position, proving the correctness of socialist ideas in practice— which means anything from a small strike to the revolution itself.

Some people see the revolutionary socialist party as the precursor of socialism. This is completely wrong. Socialism can only come about when the working class itself takes control of the means of producing wealth and uses this to transform society.

You cannot build an island of socialism in a sea of capitalism. Attempts by small groups of socialists to cut themselves off and lead their lives according to socialist ideas always fail miserably in the long term—for a start, the economic and ideological pressures are always there. And in cutting themselves off from capitalism, such small groups also cut themselves off from the only force that can bring socialism: the working class.

Of course, socialists fight against the degrading effects of capitalism every day—against racism, against sexism, against exploitation, against brutality. But we can only do so by taking the strength of the working class as our base.

11

Imperialism and national liberation

THROUGHOUT the history of capitalism the employing class has always looked to an additional source of wealth—the seizure of wealth produced in other countries.

The growth of the first forms of capitalism at the close of the middle ages was accompanied by the seizure by western states of vast colonial empires—the empires of Spain and Portugal, of Holland and France, and, of course, of Britain. Wealth was pumped into the hands of the ruling classes of western Europe, while whole societies in what is now sometimes called the 'Third World' (Africa, Asia and South America) were destroyed.

Thus, the 'discovery' of America by Europeans in the sixteenth century produced a vast flow of gold into Europe. The other side of that coin was the destruction of whole societies and the enslavement of others. For example, in Haiti, where Columbus first established a settlement, the native Harawak Indians (perhaps half a million in all) were exterminated in just two generations. In Mexico the Indian population was reduced from 20 million in 1520 to two million in 1607.

The Indian population of the West Indies and of parts of the mainland was replaced by slaves captured in Africa and transported across the Atlantic under abominable conditions. An estimated 15 million slaves survived the Atlantic crossing while about nine million died in transit. About half the slaves were transported in British ships—which is one reason why British capitalism was the first to expand industry.

The wealth from the slave trade provided the means to finance industry. As an old saying put it, 'The walls of Bristol are cemented with the blood of the negroes'—and this applied just as much to other ports. As Karl Marx put it, 'the veiled slavery of the wage worker in Europe required for its pedestal slavery pure and simple in the New World'.

The slave trade was complemented by pure looting—as when the British conquered India. Bengal was so advanced that the first British visitors were stunned by the magnificence of its civilisation. But this wealth did not stay long in Bengal. As Lord Macauley wrote in his biography of the conqueror, Clive: 'the immense population was given up as prey. Enormous fortunes were thus rapidly accumulated at Calcutta, while 30 million of human beings were reduced to the extremity of wretchedness. They had been used to living under tyranny, but never tyranny like this.'

From that point onwards Bengal became renowned not for its wealth, but for a grinding poverty that every few years saw millions starve to death in famines, a poverty that continues to this day. Meanwhile, in the 1760s at a time when total capital investment in England was no more than £6-7 million, the annual tribute to England from India was £2 million.

The same processes were at work in relation to England's oldest colony—Ireland. During the great famine of the late 1840s when Ireland's population was halved by starvation and emigration, more than enough wheat to feed the starving population was sent from the country as rent to English landlords.

Today, it is usual to divide the world into 'developed' and 'underdeveloped' countries. The impression is given that the 'underdeveloped' countries have been moving in the same direction for hundreds of years as the 'developed' countries, but at a slower speed.

But, in fact, one reason for the 'development' of the western countries was that the rest were robbed of wealth and pushed *backwards*. Many are *poorer* today than they were 300 years ago.

As Michael Barratt Brown has pointed out, 'the wealth per head of the present underdeveloped lands, not only in India, but in China, Latin America and Africa, was higher than in Europe in the seventeenth century, and fell as wealth grew in Western Europe.'

The possession of an empire enabled Britain to develop as the world's first industrial power. It was in a position to stop other capitalist states getting their hands on the raw materials, markets and profitable areas of investment within its third of the world.

As new industrial powers such as Germany, Japan and the US grew up, they wanted these advantages for themselves. They built up rival empires or 'spheres of influence'. Faced with economic crisis, each of the major capitalist powers tried to solve its problems by encroaching on the spheres of influence of its rivals. Imperialism led to world war.

This in turn produced huge changes within the internal organisation of capitalism. The tool for waging war, the state, became much more important. It worked ever more closely with the giant firms to reorganise industry for foreign competition and war. Capitalism became state monopoly capitalism.

The development of imperialism meant that capitalists did not just exploit the working class of their own country; they also took physical control of other countries and exploited their population. For the most oppressed classes in the colonial countries, this meant that they were exploited by foreign imperialists *as well as* by their own ruling class. They were *doubly exploited*.

But sections of the ruling classes in the colonial countries also suffered. They saw many of their own opportunities to exploit the local population stolen from them by imperialism. In the same way, the middle classes in the colonies, who would have liked to see a rapid expansion of

78

locally run industry so as to provide them with good career opportunities, suffered as well.

The last 60 years have seen all these various classes in colonial and ex-colonial countries rise up against the effects of imperialism. Movements have developed that have attempted to unite the whole population against foreign imperialist rule. Their demands have included:

• Expulsion of foreign imperialist troops
• Unification of the whole national territory under a single national government, as against its division between different imperialisms
• The re-establishment of the original language in everyday life, as opposed to some language imposed by the foreign rulers
• The use of the wealth produced by the country to expand local industry to bring about 'development' and 'modernisation' of the country.

Such were the demands of successive revolutionary upsurges in China (in 1912, 1923-27 and in 1945-48), in Iran (in 1905-12, 1917-21 and in 1941-53), in Turkey (after World War I), in the West Indies (from the 1920s onwards), in India (in the years 1920-48), in Africa (after 1945), in Vietnam (until the Americans were defeated in 1975), and, still today, in Southern Africa.

These movements were often led by sections of the local upper classes or middle classes, but they meant that the ruling classes of the advanced countries faced an additional opponent as well as their own working class. The *national* movement in the so-called 'Third World' challenged the imperialist capitalist states at the same time as did their own working classes.

For the working class movement in the advanced countries this had great importance. It meant that in its fight against capitalism, it had an ally in the liberation movements of the 'Third World'. So for example a Shell worker in Britain today has an ally in the liberation forces in South Africa who are fighting to take over the property which Shell owns there. If Shell can thwart the aims of the liberation movements in the 'Third World', then it will be more powerful when it comes to resisting the demands of workers in Britain.

This is true, even if the liberation movement in the Third World country does not have a socialist leadership—indeed, even if its leadership merely wants to replace foreign rule by the rule of a local capitalist or state capitalist class.

The imperialist state which is trying to smash that liberation movement is the same imperialist state that is the greatest enemy of the western worker. That is why Marx insisted that 'a nation that oppresses others cannot itself be free', and why Lenin argued for an *alliance* between the workers of the advanced countries and the oppressed people of the 'Third World', even when these had a non-socialist leadership.

This does not mean that socialists will agree with the way in which non-socialists in an oppressed country lead a national liberation struggle (any more than we necessarily agree with how a trade union leader leads a strike). But we have to make it clear *before anything else* that we support that struggle. Otherwise we can all too easily end up supporting our own ruling class against people it is oppressing.

We have to support a liberation struggle *unconditionally, before* we are entitled to criticise the way it is led.

However, revolutionary socialists in a country which is oppressed by imperialism cannot leave matters there. They have to argue, day in day out, with other people about how the struggle for national liberation should be waged.

Here, the most important points are contained in the *theory of permanent revolution* developed by Trotsky. Trotsky began by recognising that often movements against oppression are initiated by people from middle class or even upper class backgrounds.

Socialists support such movements because they aim to remove one of the burdens that weighs upon the most oppressed classes and groups in society. *But* we also have to recognise that those from the upper or middle classes cannot lead such struggles consistently. They will be afraid of unleashing a full-blooded mass struggle, in case this challenges not merely oppression from outside, but also their own ability to live by exploiting the most oppressed classes.

At a certain point they will run away from the struggle they themselves initiated, and, if necessary, unite with the foreign oppressor to smash it. At this point, if socialist, working class forces do not take the leadership of the national liberation struggle, it will be defeated.

Trotsky also made one final point. It is true that in most 'Third World' countries, the working class is only a minority, often a small minority, of the population. But it is nevertheless often quite big in absolute terms (for example in India and China it is tens of millions strong), it often creates a huge proportion of the national wealth in relation to its size, and it is concentrated in overwhelming numbers in the cities which are the key when it comes to ruling the country. So in a period of revolutionary turmoil, the working class can take the leadership of all other oppressed classes and seize control of whole countries. The revolution can be *permanent*, beginning with demands for national liberation and ending with socialist demands. But only if socialists in the oppressed country have from the beginning organised the workers on an *independent*, class basis—supporting the general movement for national liberation, but always warning that its middle class or upper class leaders cannot be trusted.

12

Marxism and feminism

THERE HAVE always been two different approaches to women's liberation—feminism and revolutionary socialism.

Feminism is the dominant influence on the women's movements which sprung up in the advanced capitalist countries during the 1960s and 1970s. It starts from the view that men always oppress women, that there is something in men's biology or psychological make-up which makes them treat women as inferior. This leads to the view that liberation is possible only by the separation of women from men—either the total separation of the feminists who seek 'liberated lifestyles', or the partial separation of women's committees, women's caucuses or women-only events.

Many of those who support this partial separation would call themselves socialist feminists. But in recent years *radical feminist* ideas of total separation have made the running inside the women's movement. Separatist ideas have ended time and again as a slightly radical wing of the social services, as with women's refuges.

This failing has led more feminists in another direction—towards the Labour Party. They believe that getting the right women in the right places, as MPs, trade union officials, local councillors, will somehow help all women to find equality.

The tradition of revolutionary socialism starts from a very different set of ideas. Marx and Engels, writing as far back as 1848, argued, first, that women's oppression did not arise from the ideas in men's heads, but from the development of private property and, with it, the emergence of a society based on classes. For them the fight for women's liberation was inseparable from the fight to end all class society—the struggle for socialism.

Marx and Engels also pointed out that the development of capitalism, based on the factory system, brought profound changes in people's lives, and especially in the lives of women. Women were brought back into social production, from which they had been progressively excluded with the development of class society.

This gave women a potential power which they had never had before. Organised collectively, women as workers had greater independence and ability to fight for their rights. This was in great contrast to their lives previously, when their main role in production, through the family, made them completely dependent on the family head—the husband or father.

From this Marx and Engels concluded that the material basis of the family, and so of women's oppression, no longer existed. What stopped women from benefiting from this was the fact that property remained in the hands of the few. What keeps women oppressed today is the way capitalism is organised—in particular the way capitalism uses a particular form of the family in order to make sure that its workers bring their children up to be the next generation of workers. It is a great advantage that while it pays men—and increasingly women—to work, women will devote their lives, unpaid, to making sure their men are fit to work in the factories and their children will grow up to do the same.

Socialism, by contrast, would see society taking on many of the family functions which weigh so heavily on women.

This didn't mean that Marx, Engels and their successors went about preaching the 'abolition of the family'. The family's supporters have always been able to mobilise many of the most oppressed women in its support—they see the 'abolition of the family' as giving their husbands licence to abandon them with the responsibility for the children. Revolutionary socialists have always tried instead to show how in a better, socialist society, women would not be forced into the miserable, cramped life provided by the present day family.

Feminists have always rejected this sort of analysis. Far from approaching women where they have the power to change the world and end their oppression—where they are collectively strong at work—they approach women as *sufferers*. Campaigns of the 1980s, for example, focussed on such issues as prostitution, rape or the threat to women and families from nuclear weapons. These all start from positions where women are weak.

Feminism starts with the assumption that oppression overrides class division. This leads to conclusions which leave class society intact while improving the position of *some* women—a minority. The women's movement has tended to be dominated by women from the 'new middle class'—journalists, writers, lecturers, higher grade white collar workers. The typists, filing clerks, machinists have got left out.

It is only during periods of radical change and revolutionary upsurge that the question of women's liberation becomes reality, not just for a minority, but for all working class women as well. The Bolshevik revolution of 1917 produced a much greater equality for women than ever known in the world before. Divorce, abortion and contraception were made freely available. Childcare and housework became the responsibility of society. There were the beginnings of communal restaurants, laundries and nurseries which gave women far more choice and control over their lives.

Of course, the fate of these advances couldn't be separated from the fate of the revolution itself. Famine, civil war, the decimation of the working class and the failure of revolution internationally meant the eventual defeat of socialism in Russia itself. The moves towards equality were reversed.

But the early years of the Soviet republic showed what socialist revolution could achieve, even in the most unfavourable conditions. Today, the prospects for women's liberation are far better. In Britain—and much the same is true of other advanced capitalist countries—two workers in every five are women.

Women's liberation can be achieved only through the collective power of the working class. This means rejecting the feminist idea of women's separate organisations. Only women and men workers acting together as part of a united revolutionary movement can destroy class society, and with it the oppression of women.

13

Socialism and war

THE PRESENT CENTURY has been a century of wars. Ten million people were killed in the First World War, 55 million in the Second, two million in the wars in Indochina. And the two nuclear superpowers, America and Russia, now possess the means to destroy the human race many times over.

Explaining this horror is difficult for those who take existing society for granted. They are driven to conclude that there is some innate, instinctive drive in human beings that leads them to enjoy mass slaughter. But human society has not always known war. Gordon Childe noted of Europe in the Stone Age: 'The earliest Danubians seem to have been a peaceful folk; weapons of war as against hunters' tools are absent from their graves. Their villages lacked military defences.' But 'in the later phases of the neolithic period armaments became the most conspicuous items...'

War is not caused by some innate human aggressiveness. It is a product of the division of society into classes. When, between 5,000 and 10,000 years ago, a class of property owners first emerged, it had to find the means to defend its wealth. It began to construct armed forces, a state, cut off from the rest of society. This then became a valuable means of further increasing its wealth, by plundering other societies.

The division of society into classes meant that war became a permanent feature of human life.

The slave owning ruling classes of ancient Greece and

Rome could not survive without continual wars which procured more slaves. The feudal lords of the middle ages had to be heavily armed in order to subdue the local serfs and to protect their loot from other feudal lords. When the first capitalist ruling classes began 300 or 400 years ago, they too repeatedly had to have recourse to war. They had to fight bitter wars in the sixteenth, seventeenth, eighteen and nineteenth centuries in order to establish their supremacy over the remnants of the old feudal rulers. The most successful capitalist countries, such as Britain, used warfare to expand their wealth, reaching overseas, looting India and Ireland, transporting millions of people as slaves from Africa to the Americas, turning the whole world into a source of plunder for themselves.

Capitalist society built itself through war. No wonder that those who lived within it came to believe that war was both 'inevitable' and 'just'.

Yet capitalism could never be based entirely on war. Most of its wealth came through exploiting workers in factories and mines. And that was something which could be disrupted by any fighting within the 'home country' itself.

Each national capitalist class wanted peace at home while waging war abroad. So while encouraging belief in 'military virtues' it also bitterly attacked 'violence'. The ideology of capitalism combines, in a completely contradictory way, exaltation of militarism and pacifist phrases.

In the present century war preparations have become more central to the system than ever before. In the nineteenth century capitalist production was based on many small firms competing with each other. The state was a relatively small body that regulated their relations with each other and with their workers. But in the present century big firms have eaten up most of the small firms, so eliminating much of the competition within each country. Competition is more and more international, between the giant firms of different nations.

There is no international capitalist state to regulate this competition. Instead, each national state exerts all the pressure it can to help its capitalists get an advantage over their foreign rivals. The life and death struggle of different capitalists with each other can become the life and death struggle of different states, each with its huge array of destructive weaponry.

Twice this struggle has led to world war. The First and Second World Wars were imperialist wars, conflicts between alliances of capitalist states over the domination of the globe. The Cold War was a continuation of that struggle, with the most powerful capitalist states lined up against each other in NATO and the Warsaw Pact.

In addition to this global conflict, many hot wars have raged in different parts of the world. Usually they have been struggles between different capitalist states over who should control a particular region, such as the Iran-Iraq war which broke out in 1980. All the major powers stoke the fires of war by selling the most sophisticated military technology to Third World states.

Many people who accept the rest of the capitalist system do not like this grim reality. They want capitalism, but not war. They try to find alternatives within the system. For example, there are those who believe the United Nations can prevent war.

But the UN is merely the arena where different states that embody the drive to war meet together. There they compare their strengths with each other, like boxers measuring up before a bout. If one state or alliance is easily more powerful than another, then both will see the pointlessness of a war whose outcome is known in advance. But if there is any doubt about the outcome, they know of only one way of settling the issue, and that is to go to war.

This was true of the two great nuclear alliances, NATO and the Warsaw Pact. Even though the West had the military edge over the Eastern bloc, the gap was not so great for the Russians to believe themselves at a hopeless disadvantage. So, despite the fact that a Third World War would wipe out most of the human race, both Washington and Moscow drew up plans for fighting and winning a nuclear war.

The Cold War came to an end with the political upheaval in Eastern Europe in 1989 and the collapse of the USSR into its constituent republics in 1991. There was then much talk of a 'New World Order' and a 'peace dividend.'

Instead, however, we have seen a succession of barbaric wars—the war of the West against its former ally Iraq, the war between Azerbaijan and Armenia in the former USSR, the horrific civil wars in Somalia and former Yugoslavia.

No sooner is one military rivalry between capitalist powers resolved than another takes its place. Everywhere, ruling classes know that war is a way of increasing their influence and blinding workers and peasants with nationalism.

You can loathe and fear war without opposing capitalist society. But you cannot end it. War is the inevitable product of the division of society into classes. The threat of it will never be ended by begging existing rulers to make peace. The armaments have to be wrested from their hands by a movement fighting to overturn class society once and for all.

The peace movements which emerged in Europe and North America at the end of the 1970s did not understand this. They fought to stop the introduction of Cruise and Pershing missiles, for unilateral disarmament, for a nuclear freeze. But they believed that the fight for peace could succeed in isolation from the struggle between capital and labour.

So they failed to mobilise the only power capable of stopping the drive towards war, the working class. Only socialist revolution can end the horror of war.

Further reading

THIS BOOK is a basic introduction to Marxism. Hopefully most readers will want to learn a lot more. One of the key features of Marxism is that people learn through struggle. When workers are fighting they can learn surprisingly rapidly. However, such spontaneous insights don't necessarily in themselves fully explain the world. Reading, discussion and debate are essential complements to the battles we engage in.

The list of titles below is provided as suggestions. You might want to follow up a particular topic that has been raised in this book, or you might want to dip into a bit of everything. Either way, if you've started to get a hang of how Marxism works, you won't want to stop.

Those titles marked '#' are short pamphlets. Any of this list can be obtained from your local socialist bookstall, or from Bookmarks (ring 081-802 6145).

Other introductions to Marxism

Can socialism come through parliament?# • Pat Stack
The struggle for workers' power# • Charlie Kimber
Why we need a revolutionary party# • Lindsey German
The communist manifesto# • Marx and Engels
Arguments for revolutionary socialism • John Molyneux
The revolutionary ideas of Karl Marx • Alex Callinicos

What is the real Marxist tradition? • John Molyneux
Marxism and the party • John Molyneux

Socialist education packs

1. Marxism and the modern world#
4. Basic ideas of Marxist economics#
5. Women's liberation and the class struggle#
6. What we mean by the 'isms'#
7. Marxism and the national question#

Marxist economics and the crisis

Wage labour and capital# • Marx
Wages, price and profit# • Marx
Why the world economy is in crisis# • Peter Green
Explaining the crisis • Chris Harman
Man's worldly goods • Leo Huberman

The Russian Revolution

Russia: The making of the revolution# • Steve Wright
Russia: How the revolution was lost# • Chris Harman
Ten days that shook the world • John Reed
Lessons of October • Leon Trotsky

The working class movement in Britain

Days of Hope: The General Strike of 1926# • Duncan
Hallas and Chris Harman
Socialism and the Labour Party# • Duncan Blackie
The changing working class • Alex Callinicos and
Chris Harman
1919: Britain on the brink of revolution •
Chanie Rosenberg

The making of the English working class • EP Thompson
Marxism and trade union struggle: the General
Strike of 1926 • Tony Cliff and Donny Gluckstein
The Labour Party: a Marxist history • Tony Cliff and
Donny Gluckstein

The international working class movement

Homage to Catalonia • George Orwell
The Comintern • Duncan Hallas.
The lost revolution: Germany 1918-23 • Chris Harman
Teamster rebellion • Farrell Dobbs
Nicaragua: What went wrong? • Mike Gonzalez
South Africa between apartheid and capitalism •
Alex Callinicos
Israel: the hijack state • John Rose
Zionism: false Messiah • Nathan Weinstock

Imperialism, the national question and the Third World

Hope amidst the horror: the socialist answer to
world hunger# • Mark O'Brien
Deflected permanent revolution# • Tony Cliff
Imperialism, highest stage of capitalism • Lenin
The rights of nations to self determination • Lenin
Permanent Revolution • Leon Trotsky

Women's liberation, racism and Ireland

The struggle for women's liberation# • Elane Heffernan
Origins of the family, private property and the state •
Engels

Sex, class and socialism • Lindsey German
Women workers and the trade unions • Sara Boston
The fight against racism# • Alex Callinicos
Racism, resistance and revolution • Peter Alexander
Staying power: black people in Britain • Peter Fryer
Ireland: why the troops must get out# • Chris Bambery
Ireland's permanent revolution • Chris Bambery
Labour in Irish History • James Connolly

Bookmarks
265 Seven Sisters Road, London N4 2DE, England
PO Box 16085, Chicago, Illinois, 60616, US
GPO Box 1473N, Melbourne, 3001, Australia

Printed and bound in Great Britain by
Cox & Wyman Ltd, Reading, Berkshire